Crime In England: Its Relation, Character, And Extent As Developed From 1801 To 1848

Thomas Plint

CRIME IN ENGLAND,

ITS RELATION, CHARACTER, AND EXTENT,

AS DEVELOPED

FROM 1801 TO 1848.

By THOMAS PLINT.

LONDON:

CHARLES GILPIN, 5, BISHOPSGATE STREET WITHOUT.

EDINBURGH: ADAM AND CHARLES BLACK.

DUBLIN: J. B. GILPIN.

1851.

CONTENTS.

THE ABSOLUTE RATIO OF CRIME TO POPU-
LATION: ITS CHARACTER AND PROGRESS,
AT DIFFERENT PERIODS, FROM 1805 TO 1848.

It is necessary to state, in the outset, that all the Tables of the proportions of crime, have sole reference to England. It would only perplex the question of ratios and causes, to bring Wales, with its peculiar industrial and social organization, into a general comparison of the English counties with each other, and with England and Wales, as a whole. It will be seen, in the sequel, that cogent reasons exist for this exclusion, and that, in fact, any comparison as to morality or immorality, betwixt county and county, based on ratios of crime, irrespective of the conditions of industrial and social organization, are perfectly futile and illusory.

Premising this, it is essential to show, distinctly, the proportions of crime to population, at different periods, in each of the several counties of England. Stress is laid upon an analysis which has reference to the counties of England *individually*, because the several questions :—
1. Whether manufactures or agriculture are most favourable to morality; 2. Whether ignorance is greater in the one section or the other; and, 3. Whether the original

relationship of feudal lord and vassal was more conducive
to national order, morality, and happiness, than the modern
arrangement of employer and employed—in other words,
than the factory system—all have been made to depend for
solution on a grouping of counties, which is most absurd
and unphilosophical. Two examples must suffice: it would
be idle to waste time in further exposure of so vicious a
principle of classification. Mr. Fletcher, one of her Ma-
jesty's Inspectors of Schools, in his elaborate but disjointed
work on the Moral Statistics of England and Wales, adopts
a classification of counties, which results in eight groups :
two only will be noticed, and they may be taken as fair
samples of the remaining six. There is first " The Northern
and Midland Mining and Manufacturing Counties" group.
The counties comprised in this group are Lancashire,
Yorkshire, Cheshire, Derbyshire, Nottinghamshire, Staffordshire, Leicestershire, Worcestershire, Warwickshire,
and Gloucestershire. In Mr. Fletcher's too elaborate
Tables, this group is continually placed in contrast with
other groups of counties, agricultural, metropolitan, &c.,
and conclusions drawn, as to the incidence of particular
social and industrial organizations, because, *on the average
of these ten counties*, certain crimes are found to preponderate, as compared with the ratio of crime in other groups
of counties, equally arbitrary in their arrangement ! To
deal with one group, is to deal with all. The grouping
is absurd, so as to be ridiculous ; has obviously been
adopted to serve a theory, and will not bear a moment's
examination. Here is the proof ! —

The 8th group of Mr. Fletcher comprises, as has been
stated, ten counties. Let it be especially noted that in
all comparisons with other groups of counties, the *average*

of crime and ignorance in those groups, is tested by the
average of crime and ignorance in the 8th group. It
might be expected that the ten counties would exhibit
something like uniformity in the ratios of crime and ignorance. Nay, they ought so to do, if the argument of Mr.
Fletcher is to be maintained; namely, "that the industrial
organization of the manufacturing districts engenders
crime." Here are the actual ratios at three distinct
periods :—

—	Number of Criminals in each 100,000 of the Population.			Ignorance as indicated by the Marriage Marks. Aver-age, 1839 to 1845.	
COUNTY.	1821.	1831.	1845.	Males in 100 Marriages.	Females in 100 Marriages.
Lancashire	169	173	161	39	67
York - -	68	97	91	w.r. 38	64
Chester -	117	161	176	36	61
Derby - -	45	86	85	30	49
Nottingham	125	141	115	34	53
Stafford -	105	154	146	43	60
Leicester -	94	105	171	33	50
Worcester -	121	145	233	45	60
Warwick -	189	204	188	32	48
Gloucester	140	208	213	29	42

Does it need more than a moment's glance at this Table,
to show that any general conclusion, as to the effect of
manufacturing and mining operations, on crime, or as to
the comparative effect on crime, of manufacturing and
agricultural occupations, derived from it, is utterly fallacious? Take 1845, and there is a minimum of crime of
85 in 100,000 of the population, and a maximum of 233,

lumped together and *averaged ;* and for the same year a
minimum, as to ignorance, of 29 marriage marks in 100,
against a maximum of 45 in 100; and what is most remarkable, the highest intelligence, as indicated by the
marriage marks, namely, in Gloucestershire, is accompanied
with the greatest ratio of crime, excepting only Worcestershire ! The West Riding of York, with 38 marriage marks,
has less than one-half the crime of Gloucestershire, in which
those marks are only 29.

The second instance is the South Midland and Eastern
Agricultural Counties Group, as under :—

—	Crime: Number of Criminals in each 100,000 of the Population.			Ignorance as indicated by the Marriage Marks. Average of 1839 to 1845.	
COUNTY.	1821.	1831.	1845.	Males in 100 Marriages.	Females in 100 Marriages.
Huntingdon	51	95	134	45	54
Norfolk -	109	128	169	44	50
Suffolk -	93	134	156	46	52
Essex - -	97	187	163	47	53
Oxford -	82	149	167	35	44
Berks - -	122	149	157	41	44
Wilts - -	108	185	152	44	54

In each year there are wide differences in the ratio of
crime, though least in the last, 1845 ; whilst there are even
greater differences in the progress of crime from one period
to another, than in the relative proportions, at each separate period.

The system of grouping counties according to some broad analogy of occupation, is, in one word, simply absurd. The only mode, in fact, on which correct conclusions can be established, is that of taking the ratios of crime at certain periods of time in each county, *separately*, and then by a comparison of counties, in which similar phases and changes of crime are discernible, to deduce broad general conclusions, *if such may be so deduced*, as to the influence, favourable or otherwise, of particular industrial organizations ; or even a better course would be to try and find out what are the real and efficient causes of crime common to all.

On this principle, the following Table is constructed :—

Table I., showing the Number of Criminals in each 100,000 of the Population of the several Counties of England, and in all England, for the undermentioned Years.

COUNTY.	1801	1820-2	1830-2	1835-7	1840-2	1845-6	1848.
Bedford . . .	31	121	117	149	183	155	173
Berks	56	122	149	147	203	157	207
Bucks. . . .	30	70	147	148	173	175	190
Cambridge . .	44	96	118	162	135	155	141
Chester . . .	41	117	161	162	256	176	241
Cornwall . . .	23	36	57	71	89	75	73
Cumberland . .	15	36	43	75	74	73	70
Derby	24	45	86	77	103	85	88
Devon . . .	27	76	92	111	132	131	164
Dorset . . .	32	60	114	126	151	118	153
Durham . . .	16	34	51	60	73	76	85
Essex	63	97	187	196	202	163	187
Gloucester .	56	140	208	210	266	213	223
Hereford . . .	34	110	136	141	238	178	232
Hertford . . .	44	97	178	199	204	154	208
Hunts. . . .	39	51	95	120	121	134	165
Kent	68	115	143	172	183	147	169
Lancashire . .	46	169	173	171	239	161	193
Leicester . . .	35	94	105	164	220	171	150
Lincoln . . .	27	67	90	118	116	117	126
Middlesex . .	148	248	261	228	238	261	277
Monmouth . .	43	68	123	112	237	165	194
Norfolk . . .	59	109	128	171	175	169	160
Northampton .	31	79	95	112	162	138	143
Northumberland	24	43	40	68	88	82	73
Notts	52	125	141	134	141	115	135
Oxford . . .	34	82	149	167	208	167	175
Rutland . . .	24	59	128	108	108	112	228
Salop	47	77	106	98	177	132	121
Somerset . . .	38	123	161	199	250	194	194
Southampton .	66	110	154	160	199	154	186
Stafford . . .	37	105	154	162	226	146	186
Suffolk . . .	51	93	134	160	157	156	151
Surrey . . .	73	128	162	183	167	150	194
Sussex . . .	64	97	117	134	182	137	170
Warwick . . .	92	189	204	213	246	188	272
Westmoreland .	15	31	39	41	63	84	82
Wilts	67	108	185	156	196	152	170
Worcester . .	36	121	145	153	258	233	272
York	27	68	97	86	133	91	114
All England. .	54	115	146	152	187	156	177

The first striking fact to notice, in connexion with this Table, is the great relative ratio of crime to population in 1845, as compared with 1801. The year 1845 (being the average of 1844-45 and 46) is selected, because it was a period uninfluenced by accidental causes of depression, which, as will be shown in the sequel, greatly affect the amount of crime. The absolute ratio of crime for all England, in 1801, is shown in the Table to have been 54 in 100,000; and in 1845, 156 in 100,000—nearly three-fold.

It is believed, that the two ratios put in juxtaposition here, represent the actual increase of crime, of which the assizes and quarter sessions take cognizance, betwixt the one and the other period. The question is quite fair and pertinent, Does the ratio of crime to population in 1845, shown by the criminal returns, as compared with 1801, indicate an actual increase of vice and criminality in the people at large, or does it simply indicate such a change in the organization of society as engenders a criminal class—which, though limited in numbers, are the actual perpetrators of the mass of offences? The solution of this question involves one of two conclusions—either that the whole mass of the people are degenerating, or that the altered organization of society, and particularly in the growth and wealth of the town population, increases the opportunities for certain classes of offences against property, and thus leads to a considerable increase of the criminal class, as distinct from all other classes, whilst the general population is growing in knowledge and morality.

To solve this question, it is necessary to look at the Table in detail. The average of increase in all England, betwixt 1801 and 1845, is, in round numbers, threefold.

It is essential to note, preliminarily, that the increase of crime, as indicated by the records of the sessions and the assizes, may not correctly measure the degree of crime at the more recent epochs, as compared with its degree at the earlier. Changes in the law, greater activity of the police, may have had much to do with the increased ratios of *detected crime;* and just so far as these may have so affected those ratios, do they lessen the proof of greater criminality amongst the general population, which those ratios seem to warrant.

It is known that in 1834 the assaults were transferred to the sessions, having previously come under the summary jurisdiction of the magistrates, thereby adding some 1400 or 1500 offences to the sum of crime in that year. There do not exist sufficient means of deciding how far the criminal roll has been swelled in this way,—nor is it perhaps of much importance, as respects the ultimate decision, as to the progress of crime. It may turn out that the ratio of criminals to the population at different periods, has little to do with the question of the greater or less morality of the mass of society.

The Table, as stated before, shows a nearly threefold ratio of crime to population, comparing 1845 with 1801. The increase is currently believed to be much greater,— that conviction arising from the exceedingly inaccurate and loose manner in which statisticians, who parade voluminous Tables of figures, calculated in the most scientific manner, put the increase of crime, relatively to the increase of population. Thus nothing is so common as to state a five or six-fold increase of crime greater than of population, within certain specified periods. Ninety-nine persons out of one hundred draw the conclusion that crime has in-

creased *relatively to the entire population*, in the same ratio
that the increase of crime within such defined periods, has
proceeded faster than the simple increment of the population. It is not so! It is incorrect to compare *the
increase of crime, simply*, with the added population.
The true method by which to indicate increasing *ratios* of
crime, or otherwise, is to place the total crime at each
period, against the total population ; and then to compare
the ratios. A simple case will show the absurdity of the
usual mode of stating the result.

The number of crimes in England in 1805 was 4527,
In 1845 (average of 1844 and 1846) it was 24,619, or
upwards of 440 per cent. increase ; and the increase of
the population being but ninety per cent., there is, apparently, an increase of 350 per cent. in crime! But the
ratio of crime to population in 1801, was 1 in 54 ;
and in 1845, 1 in 156, or less than 200 per cent.
increase! The explanation of the apparent discrepancy
is, that the ratio of the increase of crime, as compared with
the ratio of the increase of population within specified
periods ; and the ratios of the total crimes to the total
population,—are not co-equal things. The fallacy in the
process is the very obvious one of putting the entire increment of crime against the simple increment of population,
neglecting to separate from the former, so much as necessarily relates to the original quantum of the population.

This great fallacy being disposed of, the actual increase
of crime may be more carefully and accurately ascertained.
Let it be specially noticed that, in this comparison, the
ratios are solely of criminals to each 100,000 persons, in
the respective counties. The nearly threefold average,
comparing 1801 with 1845, is that of the whole of

England.   The following classification will show the differing ratios of increase, in sections of counties :—

Under 100 per cent.
    Middlesex.

100 to 150 per cent.
Kent	Sussex
Notts	Warwick
Southampton	Wilts.
Surrey	

150 to 200 per cent.
Berks	Salop
Essex	York.
Norfolk	

200 to 250 per cent.
Cornwall	Lancashire
Hertford	Northumberland
Hunts	Suffolk.

250 to 300 per cent.
Cambridge	Gloucester
Derby	Monmouth
Dorset	Stafford.

300 to 350 per cent.
    Lincoln.

300 to 350 per cent.
Northampton	Chester.

350 to 400 per cent.

Devon   Leicester

Cumberland   Oxford

Durham   Rutland.

400 to 450 per cent.

Hereford   Somerset.

Bedford

450 to 500 per cent.

Bucks   Westmoreland.

500 per cent. and upwards.

Worcester.

Nothing could more decisively set aside the entire grouping
of counties adopted by Mr. Fletcher, and in another
form by Mr. Symons, than this statement. It transposes
almost every county into a new category, and sets all their
grouping at defiance. Let it be granted, that the increase of
crime in the counties above, is not to be taken as an index
of their relative position in the total of crime, still, the questions occur, *How? Why?* is it that the increase is so much
more rapid in the counties in which crime on the whole
is the least, than in those in which, for the entire period
compared, it has been the highest?

Allowing for peculiar conditions, social and industrial,
in particular counties, such as Monmouth and Worcester—
in which mining occupations have vastly increased within
a short period of time—the great fact indicated by the
different ratios of increase, is unquestionably, that in
counties densely-populated, the incentives and occasions
of crime have nearly reached their maximum ; and that

in counties in which the population is becoming more dense—
that is, more aggregated in towns or cities—those incentives
and occasions are just beginning to be felt.

It is idle, and worse than idle, to elaborate the influence
of education, as indicated by the ratios of marriage marks,
or of the proportions of the independent classes, to all others,
*as explanatory of the differing proportions in the progress
of crime* in particular counties. Let one or two pregnant
instances suffice. Middlesex has the fewest marriage
marks, and throughout the forty-five years under review,
it has been the most criminal county in England. Gloucestershire and Worcestershire stand next as to marks, and
are next in the ratio of crime to Middlesex. In fact, there
is a gross fallacy in applying the test of the marriage marks,
and the proportion of persons of independent means, to all
the other classes, as *criteria* of ignorance or moral influences.
The simple fact indicated by the fewer marriage marks, or
the greater proportion of persons of independent means, in
particular counties, is, that the middle and upper classes
preponderate in such counties; and to draw from such proportions the inferences :—1. That the *people*, meaning
thereby the mass, are more ignorant :—and, 2. That the
presence of a higher proportion of persons of independent
means, promotes the general intelligence and morality of
the operative population—is a *non sequitur*—is absurd.
It is obvious, that if the relative proportions of the middle
and upper classes, to the *so-called* operative or working
class, were alike in all counties, the marriage marks, and
the amount of crime, would indicate the comparative degree
of instruction, and also the morality of the operative
class; because it is obvious, that in the middle and wealthy
classes, few, if any instances occur, of inability to write,

and it is also clear, from the nature of the crimes which
come before the sessions and the assizes, that the great
mass are committed by a class among the operatives ; or
rather, as will be shown in the sequel, by a criminal class,
distinct from the indigenous working population.

It will hence appear, how futile it is to attempt to draw
conclusions, as to the comparative ignorance and criminality
of particular counties, from a comparison of the ratios of
marriage marks, or of crime, simply—without first elimin-
ating, if such be practicable, the proportions of the
several classes. What is wanted to be known, is the
relative intelligence and morality of particular classes, and
this is attempted to be proved by reference to ratios,
referring *to all classes in the aggregate.* The very first
matter to ascertain is the relative proportions of the classes,
and that not being settled, the remaining parts of the
process are worthless.

Directly referring now to the classification of counties
on page 14, it is observable that there is a variation in
the progress of crime from less than 100 per cent. to
upwards of 500 per cent. What is the significance of the
variation ? Is the increase of crime greatest where the
absolute ratio of crime was greatest in 1845, or is it just
the reverse ? The following Table answers the question.
It shows the proportion of criminals to each 100,000 of
the population in 1801, and the increased ratio of crime
since 1805, in ten counties which in 1801 stood the first,
and ten counties which stood the lowest, in the order of
criminality.

Counties in which Crime was the Lowest in 1901.			Counties in which Crime was the Highest in 1801.		
COUNTY.	Ratio of Crime to 100,000 of the Pop. in 1801.	Increase of Crime, 1801 to 1845.	COUNTY.	Ratio of Crime to 100,000 of the Pop. in 1801.	Increase of Crime, 1801 to 1845.
1. Westmoreland ...	15	450 to 500	31. Gloucester ...	56	250 to 300
2. Cumberland	15	350 to 400	32. Norfolk	59	150 to 200
3. Durham	16	350 to 400	33. Essex	63	150 to 200
4. Cornwall	23	200 to 250	34. Sussex.........	64	100 to 150
5. Derby...............	24	250 to 300	35. Southampton	66	100 to 150
6. Northumberland	24	200 to 250	36. Wilts	67	100 to 150
7. Rutland...........	24	350 to 400	37. Kent	68	100 to 150
8. Lincoln	27	300 to 350	38. Surrey.........	73	100 to 150
9. York	27	150 to 200	39. Warwick......	92	100 to 150
10. Devon...............	27	350 to 400	40. Middlesex ...	143	under 100

Now, what are the inferences which this Table warrant?
Let us see. First, that crime, with one exception (York),
has increased most rapidly in those counties which were
least criminal in 1801. Second, that in the most densely
populated counties, it appears to have nearly attained
its maximum—that fact being indicated by its slow and
retarded progress in such counties; as, for instance, Middlesex, Warwick, and Surrey. Say, then, that crime is
the measure of ignorance, it is a fair inference that
ignorance is disappearing or decreasing in Middlesex and
Warwick, and increasing in Westmoreland and Cumberland! No sane person believes any such thing. It is
demonstrable that in all England, and therefore in all its
counties, education has been extended in a mighty degree;
and yet in the very counties in which, according to Mr.
Fletcher, the moral influences, as indicated by the proportion of persons of independent means, &c., are most rife,

crime has increased more rapidly than in any other! The
fact suggests that there is some disregarded element in the
question of crime.   It needs no great sagacity to discover
what that element is!   Dissect the entire crime of the
country,—what is its complexion?   In 1841, 73 per cent.
of all the crime consisted of simple larcenies and embezzlements ; and in 1845, 76 per cent.   What chance has the
perpetrator of petty larcenies in such counties as Cumberland and Westmoreland, or even Durham, compared with
counties like Lancashire, Yorkshire, Middlesex, and Warwick,
with their densely populated capitals and chief towns?   It
is rather a vague evidence of the morality of a county, that
offences are *not* committed, which, from their very nature,
must be few in it.   The pickpocket and the thief can find
no nestling-place amongst the statesmen of Cumberland and
Westmoreland, or the miners of Durham and Cornwall.
They fly to Birmingham, London, Manchester, Liverpool,
Leeds.   They congregate where there is plenty of plunder,
and verge enough to hide in.   The recognition of this
simple truth would have saved a world of discussion about
ratios of marriage marks, and the proportion of persons of
independent means in particular counties ; and would, in
fact, have reduced the question of ratios of crime, very
much to the inquiry,—What was the density of the population, its wealth and luxury?   It will be well to place
the proportions of these offences in different counties in
juxtaposition.

Percentage of Larcenies and Embezzlements in 1841 *and*
1845 *respectively, in the undermentioned Counties:*—

Counties of Least Crime in 1845.			Counties of Most Crime in 1845.		
COUNTY.	1841.	1845.	COUNTY.	1841.	1845.
1. Cumberland	71·5	72·0	31. Chester -	73·0	79·6
2. Cornwall -	73·0	73 1	32. Bucks - -	68·1	71·2
3. Durham -	68·4	62·2	33. Warwick -	77·2	77·8
4. Westmoreland	66·9	83·3	34. Oxford - -	75·9	79·7
5. Derby - -	57·2	67·1	35. Somerset -	70·2	72·4
6. York - -	68·6	71·4	36. Hereford -	76·7	71·8
7. Rutland -	62·4	66·4	37. Southampton	77·8	80·8
8. Notts - -	73·6	70·9	38. Gloucester -	76·6	80·2
9. Lincoln -	78·0	76·1	39. Worcester -	72·3	74·2
10. Devon - -	79·9	81·8	40. Middlesex -	77·2	76·5

The differences in the ratio of larcenies and embezzlements in the two groups of counties average six per
cent., taking 1841 and 1845 together. But the relative percentage of certain crimes to all other crimes in particular
counties, does not adequately show forth the true proportions of such offences. As an instance, *simple larcenies*
are 393 parts in one million persons in Durham, and 1222
parts in Middlesex; and *all other larcenies*, 36 parts in the
million to 593 respectively. All offences being *more* in
number in Middlesex than in Durham, the percentage of
offences relatively to each other remains the same; therefore the mass of the principal item of offences (larcenies) in
the more densely populated and wealthy counties, to the
mass of such offences in the thinly peopled districts, is
only correctly seen by placing together the proportions of
such offences to the population in each set of counties

respectively. The average proportion of larcenies for all England in 1845 was 873 in one million persons; and the highest and smallest ratios were as under :—

Highest Ratio of Larcenies and Serious Offences.			Lowest Ratio of Larcenies and Serious Offences.		
COUNTY.	Larce-nies.	Serious Offncs.	COUNTY.	Larce-nies.	Serious Offncs.
Middlesex - -	1222	82	Durham - -	393	86
Gloucester, in-cluding Bristol	1290	95	Northumberland	407	60
			Derby - - -	429	41
Worcester - -	1314	115	Cumberland -	424	60
Southampton -	1108	73	Cornwall - -	489	50
Warwick - -	1078	57	Notts - - -	450	56
Oxford - - -	1092	78			
Norfolk - - -	1074	135			

Whilst this Table so strikingly exhibits the immense preponderance of mere larcenies in the densely populated counties, the fact will not escape observation, that in the serious offences the disproportion is comparatively trifling.

One broad general inference lies upon the surface of the Table at page 10, and all the facts and figures stated; namely, that crime is proceeding at an exceedingly diminished ratio, relatively to population, in the most densely peopled counties—nay, in many, is actually decreasing. The next Table will place this fact beyond dispute.

Table II., showing the Increase or Decrease of Crime, relatively to Population, in the Counties of England, and for all England, in the undermentioned Periods.

COUNTIES.	1821 on 1801.	1831 on 1821.		1836 on 1821.		1845 on 1831.		1845 on 1821.	
	Inc.	Inc.	Dec.	Inc.	Dec.	Inc.	Dec.	Inc.	Dec.
	Per Cent.	Per Cent.	Per Cent.	Per Cent.	Per Cent.	Per Cent.	Per Cent.	Per Cent.	Per Cent.
Nottingham	160	12·8	...	7·7	...	...	22·6	...	8·8
Lancashire	252	2·6	...	1·3	...	...	6·4	...	5·0
Middlesex	67	5·2	...	...	8.6	Par	...	5·3	...
Surrey	80	26·5	...	43·	...	...	6·8	20·4	...
Kent	70	24·3	...	49·5	...	2·8	...	27·7	...
Bedford	300	...	3·4	23·1	...	32·5	...	28·1	...
Berks	120	22·1	...	20·5	...	5·3	...	28·6	...
York	150	42·6	...	26·4	...	...	6·2	33·8	...
Stafford	189	46·6	...	54·3	...	...	5·4	39·	...
Southampton	69	40·	...	45·4	...	Par	...	40.	...
Wilts	61	71·3	...	44·4	...	...	21·6	40·6	...
Sussex	50	22·2	...	38·1	...	17·	...	41·2	...
Chester	186	37·6	...	37·7	...	9·3	...	50·4	...
Gloucester	150	48·5	...	50·	...	2·3	...	50·7	...
Norfolk	83	17·4	...	56·8	...	32·	...	55·1	...
Somerset	228	30·8	...	61·8	...	20·5	...	57·6	...
Hertford	120	83·5	...	105·1	...	...	15·5	58·6	...
Cambridge	120	22·8	...	68·8	...	31·3	...	61·4	...
Hereford	228	23·6	...	28·1	...	30·8	...	61·8	...
Suffolk	190	44·	...	72·	...	16·4	...	67·6	...
Essex	154	92·7	...	102·	...	...	14·6	69·	...
Salop	64	37·6	...	27·2	...	24·5	...	71·3	...
Devon	178	21·	...	46·	...	42·3	...	72·3	...
Northampton	156	20·5	...	41·6	...	45·2	...	74·6	...
Lincoln	150	34·3	...	76·1	...	30·	...	74·6	...
Leicester	197	11·6	...	74·4	...	63·	...	82·	...
Derby	87	91·9	...	71·1	...	...	1·2	88·	...
Rutland	146	116·8	...	83·	...	...	12·5	89·7	...
Worcester	233	19·8	...	26·5	...	60·6	...	92·5	...
Dorset	175	90·	...	110·	...	3·5	...	96·6	...
Cumberland	140	18·	...	107.5	...	70·	...	100·	...
Cornwall	60	58·3	...	96·4	...	31·5	...	102·8	...
Oxford	143	81·6	...	103·6	...	12·	...	103·6	...
Warwick	106	4·	...	7·	...	...	6·0	...	Par.
Durham	114	50·	...	76·5	...	49·	...	123·6	...
Monmouth	57	80·8	...	64·6	...	34·1	...	142·6	...
Berks	119	110·	...	110·1	...	19·	...	150·	...
Hunts	30	86·3	...	135·3	...	41·	...	162·7	...
Westmoreland	106	25·1	...	32·	...	115·4	...	171·	...
Northumberland	80	...	7·	58·	...	207·5	...	186·	...
All England	112	26.9	...	32·1	...	6·9	...	35·6	...

Before noticing the indications of this Table, it may be well to state why the average of 1844 and 1846, say 1845, is taken as a final point of comparison betwixt 1821 (average 1820, 1821, 1822) and 1831 (average 1830, 1831, and 1832). The respective periods, in the main, were much alike as to the state of employment. To have compared 1842 and 1843, or 1847 and 1848, either with 1821 or 1831, would have been to do manifest wrong to the first-named periods; because in each there were disturbing causes at work, affecting the amount of employment, and the general condition of the people, and, as will be seen,' greatly increasing the ratio of crime. The full development of such influences will require a distinct chapter; and, therefore, for the present purpose, the facts of such influences must be assumed.

Turning to the Table, the first indications are, that, taking all England, the increase of crime relatively to population was as under for the periods named :—

1801 to 1821	- -	112·0 per Cent.
1821 to 1831	- -	26·9 ,,
1821 to 1836	- -	32·1 ,,
1821 to 1845	- -	35·6 ,,
1831 to 1845	- -	6·9 ,,
1836 to 1845	- -	2·7 ,,

The ten years, 1821 to 1831, give an increase of 26·9 per cent., and the fifteen years, 1821 to 1836, 32·1 per cent. The 24 years from 1821 to 1845, show an increase in the ratio of 35·6 per cent.; in the fourteen years from 1831 to 1845, of only 6·9 per cent.; and in the nine years from 1836 to 1845, of 2·7 per cent.

The figures show a rapidly diminishing ratio of increase. Let it be noted, that the ratios given are the simple and exact excess of crime, relatively to population, in the periods compared. Compared with 1801 to 1821, in which the increase was 112 per cent., the difference is marvellous; in fact, it shows, either that some powerful causes are in operation retarding crime, or that crime—that is, the offences which the national tribunals recognize as such—has its limits:—and that in particular localities it is approaching such limits. A few instances will suffice:—Crime in Middlesex was 261 in 100,000 persons in 1845, the average of England being 156 in 100,000 persons; and yet crime in Middlesex only showed an increase of 5·3 per cent. betwixt 1845 and 1821, and was *at par* comparing 1845 with 1831. Take Lancashire:—Crime was less in 1845 than 1821 by 5 per cent.; and in 1845, compared with 1831, by 6·4 per cent. Crime in Yorkshire was more by 33·8 per cent. in 1845 than 1821, and was less by 6·2 per cent. in 1845 than in 1831 !

A reference to the other end of the Table, shows some curious, but very suggestive facts. The 8 counties which stand first in the order of morality for 1845, in Table I., page 10, are those which show the largest increase of crime, comparing 1845 with 1821, in Table II., page 22, with three exceptions, and there is a moral in the exceptions. These are here placed in order:—

Order of Crime, 1845.	Crime to each 100,000 of the Population.	Increase or Decrease of Crime, 1845 on 1821.	
COUNTY.		Increase.	Decrease.
1. Cumberland - -	73	100·	—
2. Cornwall - - -	75	102·8	—
3. Durham - - -	76	123·6	—
4. Westmoreland -	84	171·	—
5. Derby - - - -	85	88·	—
6. York - - - -	91	33·8	—
7. Rutland - - -	112	89·7	
8. Notts - - - -	115	—	8·8
All England - -	156	35·6	

The section embraces 3 Agricultural Counties, 2 Mining Counties, and 3 mixed Manufacturing Counties; namely, Derby, York, and Notts. The lowest increase is in the 3 last; and just because those counties, in 1821, were in a great measure manufacturing, and possessing town populations, in which crime was closely approximating its maximum; whilst the others are only passing through the stages in which crime is of more rapid development.

In fact, the highest relative increase in crime is in the agricultural and mining counties. The counties of mixed manufacturing and agricultural occupation, show an intermediate ratio of increase; and nearly all the counties, densely peopled and greatly developed in manufactures, trade, and wealth, in 1821, show either an increase *below* the average of England, or not much above it,—with one exception—Warwick. The Registrar-General has shown that in 1844 and 1846, Warwick (or rather Birmingham) was suffering from great commercial

c

depression; and it is another confirmation of the idea prominently put forward in these pages, that, comparing 1845 with 1831, crime was *at par* in Warwickshire.

It may be denied here once for all, that crime is increasing amongst the general population of England, or rather shall it be put, that ignorance, vice, and immorality are on the increase amongst them? All the indications hitherto are, that crimes, that is, offences cognizable at the sessions and assizes, are mainly referable to a particular social and industrial organization of society, are committed by a comparatively small class, and do not indicate, with any accuracy, the general intelligence and morals.

The essential points to settle are, first, the quality of crime at particular periods; and second, the relative numbers of the class who commit crime, to the entire population. Now, it is notorious that the greatest increase of crime since 1821, has been in " offences against property without violence ;" that is, larcenies, embezzlements, and such offences. These spring out of a dense, wealthy, and luxurious condition of society; and as to the latter phase of the question, it is daily becoming more and more a settled conviction with all who know intimately the general condition of society, that crime is the product of a comparatively small class, and that its proportion to the general population is a most fallacious test of the general morality.

The testimony of Mr. Clay, Chaplain of Preston House of Correction, quoted by Mr. Frederic Hill, Inspector of Prisons, is very decisive on this point :— " It is very satisfactory to find, that notwithstanding there is still so much ignorance and drunkenness in the country (though much less I believe than formerly), and notwithstanding there yet remain many other causes of crime, I am of opinion, founded on many years' observation, that the amount of crime, in this part of the country at least, has diminished, and I am satisfied that the same holds good in almost every part of Great Britain; and that scarcely a greater mistake exists, than the prevailing idea that there is more crime in the country than formerly."

The evidence of Captain Willis, Chief Constable of Manchester, is equally decisive:—He says, " I have been Superintendent of Police, at Manchester, about 5½ years. During that time there has been a considerable *decrease* in crime, and a marked general improvement in the orderly conduct of the population. There are fewer ' robberies with violence ' than formerly; indeed, such offences are of rare occurrence, and when committed, it generally appears that the party was drunk at the time, and in company with women of the town. The conduct of the working classes of Manchester, since trade became bad, and commercial distress prevailed, has been highly praiseworthy. Though there has been much suffering, there has been no violence ; and except there have been more petty thefts than usual, there has been no increase of crime of any kind. These crimes have been committed chiefly by persons who, when trade is good, gain their livelihood in part by stealing. Such persons, when trade becomes bad, are, of course, the first to be dismissed from the factories, and then they depend wholly on stealing."

Both these extracts are from the 13th Report of Prisons. It will be well to contrast with them the opinions of gentlemen who dogmatise on the question of crime and its causes ; because, happily, they are in the employ of the

c 2

Commission of Council of Education and, like the inspectors
of factories, judge themselves qualified to pronounce, *ex
cathedra*, on many great social problems, on which their
chances of information are not greater than other men's,
not to say that their prepossessions are much against an
impartial judgment.

Mr. Fletcher, in page 7 of his Moral Statistics, is at
great pains to show that the statistics of children at Sunday and day schools in particular districts, indicate no
moral results.   He is at pains also to show that education
is more widely diffused in the purely agricultural counties
of the eastern and south midland parts of the nation, and
the least-educated agricultural counties, than in the manufacturing counties.   And to prove this, he produces a Table,
page 12, in which he shows that the total "increase of
education betwixt 1839 and 1844, as indicated by the
number of marriage marks in the least-instructed agricultural districts, was as 2·2 to 0·9 compared with the least-
instructed manufacturing districts;" utterly unmindful that
such an altered per centage of instructed and uninstructed,
indicates nothing more or less than the fact that the ratios
of the actually operative, the simply working class, as
compared with all other classes, have, in consequence of an
altered industrial organization, greatly changed.   Where
there is the greatest proportion of the operative classes,
there will necessarily be, all other things being alike, the
greatest proportion of marriage marks ; and Mr. Fletcher
is so ignorant of this simple principle, that without referring to anything but mere ratios of marriage marks, he
specially puts the West Riding of York and Lancashire
behind the agricultural and mining districts north of the
Humber ; and even with the least-educated agricultural coun-

ties. But Mr. Fletcher may be met on his own ground. Let crime be taken as the moral index, and let the ratio of crime in 1845 express relative ratios :—

North Midland and North Eastern Agricultural Counties.

Crime in 1845.	Number of Criminals in 100,000 of the Population.	Marriage Marks in 100 Marriages.	
COUNTY.		Males.	Females.
Lincolnshire - -	117	32	46
Shropshire - -	132	42	53

Southern Agricultural and Maritime Counties.

Devon - - -	131	28	41
Dorset - - -	118	34	43
Southampton -	154	31	39
Sussex - - -	137	30	39
Kent - - - -	147	29	39

North Midland Mining and Manufacturing Counties.

York, W. Riding	100	38	64
Lancashire - -	161	39	67
Chester - - -	176	36	61
Derby - - - -	85	30	49
Stafford - - -	146	43	60
Warwick - - -	188	32	48
Nottingham - -	115	34	53
Leicester - - -	171	33	50
Gloucester - -	213	29	42
Warwick - - -	233	45	60

Northern Agricultural and Mining Counties.

Crime in 1845. COUNTY.	Number of Criminals in 100,000 of the Population.	Marriage Marks in 100 Marriages.	
		Males.	Females.
Cumberland - -	73	16	36
Northumberland	82	19	37
Westmoreland -	84	20	35
Durham - - -	76	25	48
York, N. Riding -	78	23	40
York, East Riding	89	20	39

It is proper to state, that, in computing the crime of the
several Ridings of Yorkshire, it has been assumed, that
the East Riding will conform with Derby; York, with
Cambridge ; and the North Riding, with Durham ; leaving
all the remaining incidence of crime to fall on the West
Riding. This is unquestionably a fair apportionment,—
looking to the ratios of the criminal calendars of each
Riding, and also considering the high moral character of
the counties with which the East and North Ridings are
compared. Now what is the result of the comparison ?
The West Riding of York is scarcely 20 per cent.
higher than the most moral counties of the north, agricultural and mining ; and far below Devon, Dorset, Southampton, Sussex, and Kent! Lancashire, with its dense
population, is little above Southampton and Kent ;—
Derby ranks with the most approved counties. Nottingham
is below the entire group of the North Midland and South-

ern agricultural counties, and manufacturing Staffordshire is only a little ahead of agricultural Sussex!

Why is not education, as indicated by the marriage marks, always uniform in its effects? Why is the West Riding of York, on a most fair calculation, only a trifle above the average crime in the entire group of NORTHERN AGRICULTURAL AND MINING COUNTIES? Why is Lancashire so little above Southampton and Kent?

The simple solution of these apparent anomalies is, that the marriage marks indicate the comparative ratio of the merely operative classes to all other classes; and that the wide difference betwixt the ratios of crime in counties which exhibit the same marriage marks; or equal ratios of crime, with widely different proportions of marriage marks, indicate variations in social and industrial condition, which have far more to do with the prevalence of crime, than either the one or the other. It is sufficient to put the three following counties in juxtaposition, to destroy all reliance on marriage marks as indications of morality. The marriage marks are nearly alike: look at the ratios of crime.

	Marriage Marks. Men.	Women.	Crime, in proportion to 100,000 of the population.
Gloucester . .	29	42	213
Derby . . .	30	49	85
Sussex . . .	30	39	137

Another authority may be quoted. Mr. J. Symons in his recent work, "Tactics for the Times," is at great pains to show the high and increasing degree of criminality in the factory districts, and affirms, "that the population in them has grown up apart from the sympathies of civilisation, and are daily becoming more *vicious and heathenish*."—

Mr. Symons might have saved himself a great deal of
eloquent abuse of the factory districts, if he had carefully studied the relation of density of population to
frequency of crime ; and if he had taken the constantly
higher ratio of crime in Middlesex, as an index of the
causes which are in operation in all rapidly growing
counties, to augment crime. But Mr. Symons has no
excuse for want of exactness in his statements. On page
50, he states—that the thickly "populated districts of
Shropshire, Cheshire, Gloucestershire, Warwickshire, Staffordshire, Lancashire, Worcestershire (and *last — not
least, London itself*), though comprising little above a
quarter of the population, supply nearly *half* the crime of
the country." Now, the crime and the population of the
seven counties, excluding London, stood to each other as
follows, in 1845 and 1848 respectively :—

	1845.	Proportion to total population.	1848.	Proportion to total population.
Population	4,186,994	26·4	4,429,648	26·7
		Proportion to all crime.		Proportion to all crime.
Crime .	7,176	27·2	9,012	30·7

Now, crime and population in all England, in the same
years, stood as under :—

	1845.	1848.
Population	15,869,285	16,564,019
Crime . .	24,619	29,427

The alleged proportions of population and crime are not
found here. The population is "a little above a quarter of
the population of England ;" but the crime is not *one-third*,
instead of nearly *one half!* There is palpably a great mistake.
Mr. Symons appears to have added the crime of London

to the crime of the seven counties named, and to have forgotten to add the population! Yet on this gross arithmetical blunder, Mr. Symons gravely pronounces—"That to the evils of crowded districts and the concomitant evil of crowded dwellings and vicious companionship, *without adequate moral* counteraction, the *vast* increase of crime in England must be *primarily attributed ; for in such districts it unquestionably centres and culminates !* "

It would be .uncandid to hold Mr. Symons too closely to the result of a mere error of calculation ; but he cannot be held excused for charging on the seven counties named, the "vast *increase of crime in England,*" seeing that Lancashire shows a *decrease* of 5 per cent. comparing 1845 *with* 1821 ; that London is 5·3 per cent. less, comparing the same periods; and that of the remaining six counties, the increase is respectively—39, 50·4, 50·7, 71·4, 92·5, and 104·3 per cent., whilst there are eight purely agricultural counties, which show an increase of crime ranging from 89·7 to 186 per cent. and three mining counties which exhibit an increase of from 102 to 140 per cent.! And why exclude Nottingham and Yorkshire, in his comparison of manufacturing with agricultural counties ? Just to serve a theory, and have a fling at the manufacturing districts! The fact is, Mr. Symons, and his compeer Mr. Fletcher, have got an idea patented in their minds, that manufacturing industry divides classes, and therefore lessens the influence of the more wealthy and intelligent portion of society over the rest; and that, without such influence, there are no means of civilizing, enlightening, and moralizing the community. They are insensible to the fact, that in this very condition of society classes have sprung up, shrewd, intelligent, independent,

and exerting a great political influence ; and they know
nothing whatever of the principle which that fact indicates
and distinctly proves, that the education of a people,
moral and intellectual, needs not the appliances they
advocate, and perhaps least of all, the hot-bed appliance
of a government provision and inspectorship of education !
They may depend upon it, society in all its grades will
grow and expand, intellectually and morally, although
their calling and vocation should cease to exist ! No greater
mistake could be committed than to suppose that the intelligence and morality of a people depend simply on the
mere proportions of persons able to read and write. Education, in its widest sense, embraces all that forms men's
opinions—extends their sphere of observation and ex-
periment ; and in a free country, with a free press, there are
an infinity of causes always at work, instructing and enlightening the entire mass, far more powerful than the particular means which *they* hold as the *alone* remedy. They may
depend upon it, that it is the greatest of all mistakes to
suppose that the guiding and moulding of the national
character and will rests with a knot of educators of
children. There is a teaching of them, · by the daily
circumstances and events of life, of which these charlatans
are profoundly ignorant ; but whilst they are asleep in
their ignorance of so simple a fact, the progress of mind
and opinion is going on, and they will awake some day in
the midst of the turmoil and effervescence of general
thought, only to find that they are very bubbles on its
surface.

Having disposed of the question of the absolute ratio
of crime at different periods, and its comparative progress :
it follows in order, to notice the character of crime, at

particular periods and in particular districts. This has incidentally been adverted to, but it needs a more elaborate investigation. The Table No. III. is therefore given, and no excuse is needed on account of its voluminousness —it is full of matter for thought, and is suggestive of great facts and truths.

In this Table, a different classification of crime is adopted to that on which the Parliamentary Tables are constructed.

1. Serious Offences—not including Assaults.
2. Assaults, excluding "Assaults on the Police."
3. "Offences against Property—committed with Violence," &c.
4. "Simple Larcenies."
5. "All other Larcenies."
6. Embezzlements and Frauds.
7. Riot, Sedition, and Assaults on Police Officers.
8. All other Offences,

TABLE No. III., showing the percentage of the undermentioned
England, in the Years

COUNTY.	No. 1. Serious Offences.		No. 2. Assaults.		No. 3. Offences against property, with violence.		No. 4 Simple Larcenies.		No. 5. All other Larcenies.		Total of Larcenies.	
	1841	1845	1841	1845	1841	1845	1841	1845	1841	1845	1841	1845
Bedford	5·2	8·	·9	·1	9·1	7·4	55·5	54·	10·	13·5	65·5	67·5
Berks	3·7	4·7	2·5	1·5	9·2	5·9	58·1	62·2	8·	9·4	66·1	71·6
Bucks	4·4	5·8	·1	1·8	10·2	9·5	54·2	57·	7·6	8·2	62·	65·2
Cambridge	4.	8·2	1·7	2·2	7·7	7·2	58·9	56·7	8·1	4·5	67.	61·2
Chester	5·7	5.4	1·8	1·5	7·	5·8	57·1	60·9	8·3	12·1	65·4	73·
Cornwall	4·1	6·8	6·	3·5	3·8	2·5	64·	63·9	4·9	3·6	68·9	67·5
Cumberland	4·6	8·	4·	2·1	3·1	6·	62·	57·	5·4	5·	67·4	62·
Derby	6·5	5·	3·	2·5	16·5	10·4	43·6	50·3	7·5	12·	53·1	62·3
Devon	3·5	5·4	1·1	1·1	3·7	4·6	65·2	68·6	8·2	7·8	73·4	76·4
Dorset	4·7	6·8	1·6	3·1	7·5	4·5	64·5	63·9	2·4	7·2	66·9	71·1
Durham	8·3	11·3	3·4	4·9	7·5	6·3	53·3	50·3	6·8	4·9	60·1	55·2
Essex	4·5	7·3	1·5	1·5	9·	9·	52·6	54·5	18·3	15·3	70·9	69·8
Gloucester	3·3	4·3	2·1	1·5	5·2	4·7	60·6	57·7	11·5	15·8	72·1	73·5
Hereford	3·3	4·3	1·1	1·8	10·8	11·1	62·4	58·4	9·5	9·1	71·9	67·5
Hertford	3·2	6·	1·3	1·2	6·8	6·7	57·1	57·6	11·7	12·6	68·8	70·2
Hunts	9·	6·	3·	3·7	7·5	4·8	58·	61·4	7·5	6·	65·5	67·4
Kent	4·2	5·1	2·3	3·1	6·6	6·2	56·8	55·6	14·3	17·3	71·1	72·9
Lancaster	3·6	4·1	2·4	2·6	8·	6·4	4·7	52·9	14·5	17·2	61·2	70·1
Leicester	5·r	4·8	1·6	3·	8·4	8·8	57·9	60·	8·2	10·4	66·1	70·4
Lincoln	4·	4·5	2·	1·8	6·5	7·	68·7	64·8	3·3	4·8	72·	69·6
Middlesex	2·8	3·1	5·2	7·3	4·3	3·5	50·4	47·2	20·	23·	70·4	70·2
Monmouth	4·7	5·8	2·3	1·2	6·4	6·1	56·7	62·8	8·6	9·1	65·3	71·9
Norfolk	4·5	8·	1·4	1·4	7·2	5·8	64·8	63·2	6·8	7·	71·6	70·2
Northampton	3·8	6·5	1·8	2·	7·	5·8	54·7	63·1	6·2	7·5	60·9	70·6
Northumberld..	4·3	7·3	3·5	2·6	9·2	7·3	53·4	49·9	11·2	13·5	64·6	63·4
Nutts	4·	6·6	1·4	2·5	7·1	9.	64·5	53·8	5·1	14·1	69·6	67·9
Oxford	2·8	4·6	2·1	1·4	7·6	5·7	58·9	65·4	8·5	7·8	67·4	73·2
Rutland	6·	7·5	5·	1·	11·9	11·2	45·	57·9	8·7	7·5	53·7	65·4
Salop	5·3	4·1	1·7	1·7	7·5	4·6	62·7	70·3	7·	7·	69·7	77·3
Somerset	3 8	4·5	3·3	3·3	8·7	7·4	55·5	57·6	8·	8·1	63·5	65·7
Southampton	4·1	4 6	2·7	1·5	4·7	6·3	68·6	72·3	4·	4·	72·6	76·2
Stafford	6·1	6·1	2·1	2·6	10·8	4·5	54·3	63·	5·4	9·9	59·7	72·9
Suffolk	2·5	10·	1·5	·8	8·	7·8	67·8	61·	6·4	5·8	74·2	66·8
Surrey	4·	5·	3·3	3·7	6·7	5·1	53·4	51·5	15·8	17·	69·2	68·5
Sussex	3·3	4·4	3·3	1·7	7·4	5·2	53·	53·2	12·4	16·9	65·4	70·1
Warwick	3·	2·9	·7	1·8	9·8	8·	58·	57·7	14·	14·0	72·	71·7
Westmoreland..	2·6	6·	·2	...	14·	4·	53·4	77·1	8·1	2·2	61·5	79·3
Wilts	4·4	5·5	1·4	2·5	6·4	5·3	63·6	63·	8·5	9·6	72·1	72·6
Worcester	5·2	4·8	2·3	2·1	8·3	16·7	57·8	56·7	9·9	13·5	67·7	70·2
York	4·	5·8	1·4	2·	11·4	10·	52·1	53·8	11·	12·5	63·1	66·3
All England	4·	5·1	2·5	2·9	7·5	6·1	54·9	56·4	12·3	13·8	67·2	70·2
Lowest	2·5	2·9	·1	·1	3·1	2·5	45·	47·2	2·4	2·2	53·1	55·2
Highest	9·	11·3	6·	7·3	16·5	11·2	68·6	77·1	20·	23·	74·2	79·3

lasses of Crime in the several Counties of England, and for all 1841 and 1845, respectively.

No. 6. Embezlements and frauds.		No. 7. Riot, Sedition, &c.		No. 8. All other Offences.		Total Larcenies and Embezlements		Total of Serious Offences.		All other Offences.		TOTAL.		
1841	1845	1841	1845	1841	1845	1841	1845	1841	1845	1841	1845	1841	1845	
·8	5·	7·7	5·8	5·8	6·2	71·1	72 5	5·2	8·	23·5	19·5	100	100	Bedford.
·6	6·2	5·	5·	5·9	5·1	73·7	77·8	3·7	4·7	22·6	17·5	100	100	Berks.
·1	6·	5·4	4·3	11·8	7·4	68·1	71·2	4·4	5·8	27·5	23·	100	100	Bucks.
·1	4·8	6·5	8·2	7·	8·2	73·1	66·	4·	8·2	22·9	25·8	100	100	Cambridge.
·6	6·1	7·2	4·2	5·3	3·5	73·	79·6	5·7	5·4	21·3	15·	100	100	Chester.
·1	5·6	7·5	8·5	5·6	5·6	73·	73·1	4·1	6·8	22·9	20·1	100	100	Cornwall.
·1	10·	8·3	7·3	8·	4·6	71·5	72·	4·6	8·	23·9	20·	100	100	Cumberland.
·1	4·8	9·7	8·0	7·1	7·	57·2	67·1	6·5	5·	36·3	27·9	100	100	Derby.
·5	5·4	5·6	2·5	6·2	4·6	79·9	81·8	3·5	5·4	16·6	12·8	100	100	Devon.
·4	6·4	2·4	1·4	7·5	6·7	76·3	77·5	4·7	6·8	19·	15·7	100	100	Dorset.
·3	7·	5·	11·3	7·4	4·	68·4	62·2	8·3	11·3	23·3	26·5	100	100	Durham.
·5	5·4	2·4	2·	5·2	5·	77·4	75·2	4·5	7·3	18·1	17·5	100	100	Essex.
·5	6·7	1·7	2·1	11·1	7·2	76·6	80·2	3·3	4·3	20·1	15·5	100	100	Gloucester.
·8	4·3	1·8	2·5	6·3	8·5	76·7	71·8	3·3	4·3	20·	23·9	100	100	Hereford.
·3	4·7	3·9	3·2	10·7	8·	74·1	74·9	3·2	6·	22·7	19·1	100	100	Hertford.
·	7·3	3·	6·	6·	4·8	71·5	74·7	9·	6·	19·5	19·3	100	100	Hunts.
·1	5·1	4·1	2·3	6·6	5·3	76·2	78·	4·2	5·1	19·6	16·9	100	100	Kent.
·8	8·	9·9	4·9	6·1	3·9	70·	78·1	3·6	4·1	26·4	17·8	100	100	Lancashire.
·2	6·	5·6	2·	7·1	5·	72·3	76·4	5·	4·8	22·7	18·8	100	100	Leicester.
·	6·5	4·4	2·6	5·1	8·	78·	76·1	4·	4·5	18·	19·4	100	100	Lincoln.
·8	6·3	4·1	4·	6·4	5·6	77·4	76·5	2·8	3·1	20·	20·4	100	100	Middlesex.
·8	3·8	9·1	6·1	6·4	5·1	71·1	75·7	4·7	5·8	24·2	18·5	100	100	Monmouth.
·	7·	3·	1·5	6·3	6·1	77·6	77·2	4·5	8·	17·9	14·8	100	100	Norfolk.
·1	4·	13·8	3·3	4·6	7·8	69·	74·6	3·8	6·5	27·2	18·9	100	100	Northampton.
·4	5·8	6·	5·8	6·	7·8	71·	69·2	4·3	7·3	24·7	23·5	100	100	Northumberld.
·	3·	7·1	3·	6·8	8·	73·6	70·9	4·	6·6	23·4	22·5	100	100	Notts.
·5	6·5	5·5	4·3	6·1	4·3	75·9	79·7	2·8	4·6	21·3	15·7	100	100	Oxford.
7	1·	6·	11·2	8·7	2·7	62·4	66·4	6·	7·3	31·6	26·1	100	100	Rutland.
·8	5·5	5·5	0·8	4·5	6·	75·5	82·8	5·3	4·1	19·2	13·1	100	100	Salop.
·7	6·7	6·7	5·2	7·3	7·2	70·2	72·4	3·9	4·5	26·	23·1	100	100	Somerset.
·2	4·5	5·5	3·2	4·9	3·6	77·8	80·8	4·4	4·6	17·8	14·6	100	100	Southampton.
·2	5·9	11·1	4·5	6·	3·5	63·9	78·8	6·1	6·1	30·	15·1	100	100	Stafford.
·	6·	3·	3·6	3·8	5·	81·2	72·8	2·5	10·	16·3	17·2	100	100	Suffolk.
·2	5·5	3·6	2·7	6·	9·5	76·4	74·	4·	5·	19·6	21·	100	100	Surrey.
6	8·	4·4	5·5	8·6	5·1	73·	78·1	3·3	4·4	23·7	17·5	100	100	Sussex.
2	6·1	2·5	3·9	6·8	5·6	77·2	77·8	3·	2·9	13·8	19·3	100	100	Warwick.
4	4·	10·9	6·	5·4	·7	66·9	83·3	2·6	6·	30·5	10·7	100	100	Westmoreland.
8	5·8	4·1	2·8	5·8	5·5	77·9	78·4	4·4	5·5	17·7	16·1	100	100	Wilts.
6	4·	5·4	3·	6·5	5·2	72·3	74·2	5·2	4·8	22·5	21·	100	100	Worcester.
5	5·1	7·6	5·	7·	5·8	68·6	71·4	4·	5·8	27·4	22·8	100	100	York.
6·	6·0	4·		6·8	5·7	73·2	76·2	4·	5·1	22·8	18·7	100	100	All England.
1·	1·7		·8	3·8	·7	57·2	6?·2	2·5	2·9	16·3	12·8	100	100	
10.	13·8	11·3		11·8	9·5	81·2	83·3	9·	11·3	31·6	27·9	100	100	

Two periods only are given, and those were respectively periods of Prosperity and Depression, — purposely so selected, for reference in another Chapter. The Table shows the percentage of each class of crime in each year. Under each section, there is room for copious comment. One broad general observation may be commenced with. Taking the entire 40 counties, the proportions of the 9 classes of offences, to the total of all offences, vary, comparing county with county, within very narrow limits. There is no violent excess of particular crimes in any county—excepting that in periods of distress—sedition, riot, and breach of the peace greatly preponderate over the average of ordinary crime, in the manufacturing counties. It would seem as if the tendencies to crime of particular kinds, were uniform in their ratios, at the same periods, in counties of similar organization. At different and distant periods of time, the ratios of particular crimes to each other may be greatly altered; but at the *same moment of time*, in counties generally homogeneous in social and industrial structure, the tendencies to crime of particular classes seem to maintain great uniformity. This fact unquestionably indicates the relative force of the inducement and incentives to crime, and of the *power of resistance*,—whether that be the fear of punishment, or moral principle. It would seem as if the relative proportions of crimes of particular kinds might be determined on some analogous principle, to that on which the ratios of particular diseases and of deaths to the general population, are predicted with almost unerring certainty; always bearing in mind that in the latter case the law is physical, and in the former, moral.

Passing to the Table, the small proportion of the "Serious

Offences," Class 1, to all others, demands first attention. Happily for society, the incentives to such crimes are not of every-day occurrence, and the restraints are powerful. It will be observed that the serious offences constitute a larger percentage of all offences in 1845 than in 1841; but it would be an error thence to conclude, that such offences were more rife in 1845 than in 1841. The fact is, that the "Serious Offences" were as 76 to one million inhabitants in 1841, and 77 to one million in 1845. Class 2, Assaults, needs only a passing notice. It is obvious this class of offences will be most abundant, where men meet often, and under excitement. It would be singular, if the widely-separated inhabitants of Westmoreland and Cumberland came into collision as often as the jostling inhabitants of Middlesex! Class 3, "Offences against Property, with Violence," shows, as might be expected, that in the densely peopled counties, under efficient police, such crimes are in smaller ratio than in the less-peopled counties. Class 4, "Simple Larcenies," shows, singularly enough, a greater proportion of these to all other offences, in the agricultural counties than the manufacturing; but the next, Class 5, "All other Larcenies," including those by servants in dwelling-houses, and *larcenies from the person*, exhibits a contrary aspect. The "Total of Larcenies," determines the prevailing character of crime in England, showing 67·2 per cent. in 1841, and 70·2 per cent. in 1845. Class 6, "Embezzlements," shows, as might be surely predicated, that such offences are most abundant where offices of trust and confidence are most numerous. Class 7, "Riot, Sedition, &c.," shows how, in periods of depression, the proportion of such offences increases in the manufacturing counties. The following statement abundantly proves this :—

Percentage of Riot, Sedition, &c.

COUNTIES.	1841.	1845.
Chester	- 7·2	- 4·2
Lancaster	- 9·9	- 4·9
Leicester	- 5·6	- 2·0
Monmouth	- 9·1	- 6·1
Stafford	- 11·1	- 4·5
York	- 5·4	- 3.

The only exception is Warwick, which, in 1841, was 2·5, and in 1845, 3·9 per cent. of such offences; the explanation of the apparent anomaly being that, from peculiar causes, Warwick suffered more in 1845 than 1841, contrary to the general experience of the country. The 8th Class needs no remark; but the " Total of Larcenies and Embezzlements" demands the passing observation, that such offences constitute the *staple* of crime in England ;—serious and all other offences being but 26·8 per cent. of *all* crime in 1841, and 23·8 in 1845.— This fact indicates with precision the essential nature of crime in England—*it is crime against property, in the various forms of larceny, embezzlement, and fraud*— crimes which in a wealthy and luxurious country like England, must be in the ascendant.

The effect of seasons of scarcity, and consequent distress amongst the working classes, on the ratios of particular crimes, will be noticed in the next Chapter. The relative proportion of particular classes of crime, in the manufacturing and the agricultural counties, respectively, will also be noticed in a separate Chapter.

INFLUENCE OF VARIATIONS IN THE PRICE OF FOOD, ON THE RATIO OF CRIME.

ONE great source of error in estimating the absolute ratio, the progress and the character of crime, has been the neglect to eliminate, most carefully and accurately, the effects of variations in the amount of employment for labour; or, in other words, of full employment and good wages, on the one hand—and of deficient employment and low wages, on the other.

Many elaborate articles in the STATISTICAL JOURNAL, of which the object was to prove the great and steady increase of ignorance and immorality among the general population, and much eloquent declamation in the pages of Mr. Fletcher and Mr. Symons, lose all their point and significance, when tested by the ratios of crime in years of great depression and of great prosperity, respectively. The one idea of the writers in each case was, that ignorance is the efficient cause of crime; and as crime increased at a greatly accelerated speed from 1836 to 1843, the conclusion was leaped to, that ignorance was also increasing, and in the same ratio. Some notice was indeed bestowed on the fact of oscillations in the annual total of criminal offences; but it was only to afford an opportunity to record the now stereotyped axiom of the whole school, that "although the wave of ignorance and crime had its occasional recoil, it was only to advance again with augmented force." These gentlemen ought to have been wiser than to use *figures of rhetoric*, in place of an exhaustive analysis of figures literal.

The cardinal cause of crime, according to them, is ignorance! Grant the theory — very well! Does ignorance, as pervading an entire community, rise and fall — to use their favourite metaphor? Does it move onwards in *waves?* or does it alter its proportions slowly, but by equable movements, in the one or the other direction; that is—either as diminishing or increasing? Need it be demonstrated, that no *sudden change* in the relative ignorance and wisdom of a nation is possible? The intelligence of a people is simply the aggregate intelligence of the units—the individuals of whom it consists. These units, considered intellectually, do not materially alter, year by year. The crime of a nation is committed principally by persons from fifteen to thirty years of age; and it must be obvious, from the very nature of all intellectual and moral influences, that these cannot so change the moral character of a population betwixt one year and another, as to cause the violent oscillations in the total of crime, which are patent on the face of the criminal records, for the last fifteen years! Indeed, the very fact of oscillation, on so large a scale, ought to have suggested to these parties, the unsoundness of their theory. Intellectual and moral changes, in an entire people, are, at all times, slow; and there is, at any and every moment, a certain definite tendency, either one

way or the other, for good or for ill; but it will be by
slow steps. The mind and heart of a nation is the mind
and heart of its population from twenty to fifty years of
age. The composition of this class can alter only slowly.
It requires thirty years to change *all* its elements, and it
is obvious, that the primary element of change will be the
influx of new blood,—those of the population who are
successively arriving at the age of twenty. Supposing the
intellectual and moral character of all under twenty years
of age, in a particular country, to be vastly higher
in grade than that of the population above twenty;.
the general character of the population, as indicated by
its criminal records, its political action, its literature, its
benevolent efforts or its religious fervour, could only be
slowly affected and transmuted for the better; and it is
clear, that the process of change would be that of a steady,
but almost imperceptible ascent. Violent oscillation is on
the supposition impossible; and it is proof positive of the
blinding influence of theory, that men, accustomed to a
minute examination of our criminal records, should never
have had any misgivings as to the soundness of their
theory, when the phenomena before them were so clearly
and unequivocally unconformable to the cause assigned.

To deny the process of another's argument is not,
however, to prove one's own; and it is freely acknowledged
that, unless a clear connexion can be established, betwixt
the violent oscillations alluded to, and a cause, which is
not ignorance or cognate to it, the theory, that ignorance
is the sole and efficient cause of crime, is not disproved;
though it is not, therefore, necessarily established as true;
no more than a prisoner's innocence of an alleged crime
is proved, because the evidence falls short of bringing the

crime home to him. It is proposed to show that certain
variations in the price of food, and concomitant variations
in the amount of employment for labour, are always
accompanied by an increase in the number of criminals
committed. It is further proposed to show that, in the
circumstances indicated, the marriages invariably fall off,
in a proportionate ratio to the increase on the price of food,
and the increase in the number of commitments for crime.

The fact of connexion betwixt the condition of the
people, as to employment, &c., and the number of marriages, was first distinctly pointed out in the 8th Annual
Report of the Registrar-General; and in the 9th Annual
Report, the connexion of crime with the same fact was
briefly alluded to. But the direct and powerful influence
which variations in the quantity of food, and by consequence, variations in the amount of employment for labour,
exercise, in augmenting or diminishing crime, are not
elaborated. The materials, however, for such elaboration,
are in part furnished by the Registrar-General, and in
part by the criminal returns.

The criminal Tables only allow the examination to be
carried back to the commencement of the present century,
though, as respects the marriages, the most clear and
convincing proof might be quoted, that dear food invariably checks them. The effects of that condition is, however, so distinctly shown by the marriage and the
criminal returns, since 1805, as completely to establish
the principle enunciated.

Table IV., *showing the Price of Wheat, the Number of Criminals, and the Number of Persons married in each Year, from 1805 to 1846.*

YEAR.	Price of Wheat per Quarter.			Crime.	Persons Married.
	£	s.	d.		
1805	4	9	9	4,605	159,172
1806	3	19	1	4,346	161,508
1807	3	15	4	4,446	167 846
1808	4	1	4	4,735	164,496
1809	4	17	4	5,330	166,738
1810	5	6	5	5,146	168,940
1811	4	15	3	5,337	172,778
1812	6	6	6	6,576	164,132
1813	5	9	9	7.164	167,720
1814	3	14	4	6,390	185,608
1815	3	5	7	7,818	199,888
1816	3	18	6	9,091	183.892
1817	4	16	11	13,932	176,478
1818	4	6	3	13,567	185,558
1819	3	14	6	14,254	191,142
1820	3	7	10	13,710	193,666
1821	2	16	1	13,115	201,736
1822	2	4	7	12,241	197,756
1823	2	13	4	12,263	203,836
1824	3	3	11	13,698	209,446
1825	3	8	6	14.437	220,856
1826	2	18	8	16,164	209,882
1827	2	18	6	17,294	214,260
1828	3	0	5	16,564	222,348
1829	3	6	3	18,675	208,632
1830	3	4	3	18,107	215,438
1831	3	6	4	19,647	224,588
1832	2	18	8	20,829	233,208
1833	2	12	11	20,072	240,254
1834	2	6	2	22.451	243,768
1835	1	19	4	20,731	239,196
1836	2	8	6	20,984	241,698
1837	2	15	10	23,612	228,748
1838	3	4	7	23,094	236,134
1839	3	10	8	24,443	246,332
1840	3	6	4	27,187	245,330
1841	3	4	4	27,760	244,992
1842	2	17	3	31,309	237,650
1843	2	10	1	29,591	247,636
1844	2	11	3	26,542	264,498
1845	2	10	10	24,303	287,486
1846	2	14	8	25,107	291,328

It is not to be expected that the effects of periods of
scarcity on the one hand, or of abundance on the other,
should manifest themselves with instant precision and
force.   In other words, it is not in the nature of the
cause, that the effect should be visible the moment the
cause begins to act.   The whole power of the steam is
completely shut off some time before the velocity of a train
is checked ; and, *vice versâ*, the whole power of the loco-
motive is in play, simultaneously with the just creeping
motion of its load.   By parallelism, the preceding Table
does not exhibit, in juxtaposition, year by year, variations
in the price of corn, and exactly corresponding variations
in the number of marriages and the number of criminal
offences ; but it does incontestably exhibit the unfailing
action of a *continued high price of food*, to *increase crime
and diminish marriages ;* and *vice versâ*, of a continued low
price of food, to decrease crime and increase the marriages.
Turning to the Table, the following are the most conspicuous instances of the operation of the law :—The years 1805,
1806, and 1807, show a *descending price* of food and of
crime, and an ascending number of marriages.   The price
of food rose violently in 1812, as compared with 1811, and
the number of crimes rose as violently, whilst the number
of marriages sunk in a corresponding degree.   The years
1814 and 1815, in which food was little more than half its
price in 1812 and 1813, exhibit an extraordinary increase
in the number of marriages, and a great decline in crime
for 1814, followed by a considerable increase in 1815.   The
latter fact may appear to contradict the theory advanced.
It is in appearance only.   At this particular moment, from
some unexplained cause, crimes, or rather offences, augmented in number.   From 1805 to 1815, the average

annual number of offences was 5407. In 1815, the number was 7818; in 1816, 9091; and in 1817, 13,932. It is inconceivable that this rise could be the effect of a corresponding change in the morality of the nation. It is true that, about this time, a large number of men, not of the purest morals, were dismissed from the Army and Navy; but the comparative steadiness of crime from 1817 to 1825, leaves little room to doubt that there must have been some great changes in the law at that time, either creating new classes of crime, or bringing certain crimes within the cognizance of the assizes and quarter sessions, which were previously disposed of in another manner. The anomaly merits an investigation into the history of criminal jurisprudence for the period in question, which it is hoped some qualified person will undertake. If, as seems probable, the great rise originated in changes as respects the administration of law, a great question in the history of the national morals will be solved, though at the expense of depriving certain lachrymose and declamatory writers of a fertile topic. But this is somewhat digressing.

Pursuing the examination of the Table, the years 1817 to 1819, stand in contrast with 1820 to 1823, and support the principle under consideration. The contrast will best appear in averages :—

DEAR YEARS, 1817 to 1819.			CHEAP YEARS, 1820 to 1823.		
Average price of Wheat.	Average of Crime.	Average of Marriages.	Average price of Wheat.	Average of Crime.	Average of Marriages.
£4 4 5	13,917	184,392	£2 15 5	12,832	199,248

These figures need no comment. Two other periods may be advantageously contrasted :—

YEARS.	DEAR YEARS.			YEARS.	CHEAP YEARS.		
	Average price of Wheat.	Avrg. of Crime	Average of Marrigs.		Average price of Wheat.	Avgr. of Crime	Average of Marrigs
1827 to 1831	£3 3 2	18,057	217,053	1832 to 1835	£2 4 3	21,020	239,106
1838 to 1843	3 2 2	27,230	243,012	1844 to 1846	2 12 3	25,320	281,104

There is, in the greater crime of the cheap years 1832 to 1835, an apparent contradiction to the theory advanced. It is only apparent. The ratio of crime to population was rapidly on the increase throughout the whole period from 1817 to 1831. The ratio of increase from 1832 to 1835 was much less. It is necessary therefore, in order to ascertain the exact incidence of cheaper food, in diminishing crime, to determine the incidence of *some other cause*, then operating in the contrary direction. The latter is not easily appreciable, but an approximation may be made. The increase of crime from 1827 to 1831, being the dear years, was, in round numbers, 2400, comparing the first and the last year, or about 14 per cent. Supposing the same cause to continue in operation from 1832 to 1835, being the cheap years, 1835 should have shown a total of 22,395, whereas, it was only 20,731. The rapid rise to 23,612, only two years later, as the concomitant of a great rise in the price of wheat, goes to prove the correctness of this reasoning ; because the sudden cessation of the upward tendency in crime, during the cheap years, was followed by a violent leap, immediately on the recurrence of dearness. The inference is fair and legitimate, that the retarding force from 1832 to 1835, was the abundance and cheapness of food.

If the facts stated do not conclusively establish the general propositions that dear food and increasing crime, and cheap food and diminishing crime, are respectively convertible terms, it is difficult to say what amount of evidence will suffice to establish any proposition. Be that proposition, however, admitted or not, the fact of coincidence remains indisputable, and it is at least relevant to show what is the precise degree of variation in the total amount of crime for the whole kingdom, and also whether that variation is uniform throughout all the counties, or varies more or less in its intensity, correspondingly with certain variations of social or industrial organization. For this purpose, the following Table has been constructed, which will require a particular explanation.

The object of the Table is to show, in juxtaposition, the ratio of crime in certain dear and cheap years respectively, and to measure the influence of dearness and cheapness of food respectively, on the amount of crime. For this pur. pose, two periods under each class have been selected ; namely—as periods of cheap food, 1835 to 1837, and 1844 to 1846 ; and as periods of dear food, 1840 to 1842, and 1848. The ratio of criminality is first shown for each averaged period, and the difference betwixt the several periods is indicated in columns, the headings of which convey all the explanation needed.

Table No. V., showing the Proportion of Criminals to the Population in the undermentioned Years, and the Increase or Decrease of Crime betwixt the several Periods.

COUNTIES.	Criminals 1835-7 one in	Criminals 1840-2 one in	Criminals 1844-6 one in	Criminals 1848 one in	Difference of Crime in the Years compared.			
					1840-2 more than 1835-7.	1840-2 less than 1835-7.	1848 more than 1844-6.	1848 less than 1844-6
					Per Cent.	Per Cent.	Per Cent.	Per Cent.
Bedford	669	545	645	578	22·8	...	11·6	...
Berks	693	491	634	482	38·	...	31·6	...
Bucks	675	577	564	525	16·8	...	8·6	...
Cambridge	616	705	642	736	...	20·	...	9·9
Chester	645	387	569	415	58·	...	37·	...
Cornwall	1408	1118	1317	1360	25·4	...	...	2·8
Cumberland	1317	1348	1355	1417	...	1·2	...	4·1
Derby	1286	965	1168	1134	33·6	...	3·5	...
Devon	898	755	766	609	18·8	...	26·	...
Dorset	792	658	846	653	19·8	...	39·	...
Durham	1642	1494	1305	1168	21·6	...	13·	...
Essex	510	495	610	532	3·1	...	14·6	...
Gloucester	475	375	469	448	26·6	...	4·6	...
Hereford	707	420	561	430	68·7	...	30·4	...
Hertford	502	490	647	480	2·5	...	35·	...
Hunts	833	824	742	603	·8	...	23·1	...
Kent	579	545	680	592	6·4	...	15·	...
Lancaster	582	417	621	517	40·	...	20·	...
Leicester	609	454	576	666	34·1	...	...	14·
Lincoln	845	859	851	793	...	1·8	7·7	...
Middlesex	437	420	384	361	4·3	...	6·1	...
Monmouth	887	421	605	519	111·5	...	10·8	...
Norfolk	584	570	589	623	2·3	...	...	5·6
Northampton	893	617	722	699	44·6	...	3·6	...
Northumberland	1460	1127	1209	1356	29·1	...	...	14·0
Notts	744	707	869	740	5·2	...	17·4	...
Oxford	598	478	598	569	24·5	...	4·8	...
Rutland	924	926	886	438	Par	Par	117·8	...
Salop	1013	563	749	822	80·6	...	...	9·
Somerset	502	400	516	518	25·5	...	Par	Par
Southampton	624	503	648	537	24·3	...	20·7	...
Stafford	614	441	687	537	39·5	...	27·2	...
Suffolk	624	634	638	659	...	1·9	...	3·2
Surrey	545	597	664	514	...	9·5	29·3	...
Sussex	739	550	728	588	35·8	...	24·	...
Warwick	468	405	529	367	15·5	...	44·6	...
Westmoreland	2423	1568	1187	1221	53·8	...	...	2·4
Wilts	639	510	615	586	25·3	...	11·6	...
Worcester	659	388	428	367	68·6	...	16·7	...
York	1155	750	1088	873	54·6	...	25·3	...
All England	657	533	641	562	23·	...	13·4	...

The Table shows that crime was more rife in the years 1840 to 1842, when wheat averaged 62*s*. 10*d*. per quarter, than in 1836 to 1837, when the average price was 47*s*. 10*d*. per quarter, by 23 per cent. ; and that crime was more rife in 1848, when wheat was 52*s*.* per quarter, than in 1844 to 1846, when it was 52*s*. 3*d*. per quarter. It will be seen presently, on a comparison of 1841 to 1843 (years in which crime arrived at its highest point) with 1844 to 1846, that crime was 24 per cent. higher in the former than in the latter years.

This is unquestionably a great fact. An addition of nearly *one-fourth* to the ordinary amount of crime, as the consequence of *dear food* and *deficient employment* for the masses,—two circumstances always concurrent, and, in fact, *cause and effect*, accompanied as it must be with greatly increased local and general expenditure in the administration of the law—with most painful social and domestic evils, and leaving behind it, even when better times come, as the trail of the moral wrongs which it evidences, a lowered and more degraded moral condition, at least of those who have been the subjects of judicial punishment,—is a great national calamity.

The extent of the calamity is not, however, accurately measured by the average excess of criminality on the whole of England. Referring to the Table, it will be evident that the incidence of dear food in augmenting crime, is greatest in the most densely peopled, the manufacturing and mining districts. That increase is as follows :—

* It is needful to state here, that the principal cause of the increase of crime in 1848 was the severe distress arising from the interruption of trade, caused by the revolution of February. This acted on *employment* just as a high price of food does, and it is this *ultimate* action, common to both, which is the real evil.

COUNTIES.	DIFFERENCE OF CRIME.		
	1840-2 more than 1836-7.	1848 more than 1844-6.	1848 less than 1844-6.
Cheshire (manufacturing) - - -	58·	37·	...
Cornwall (mining) - - - -	25·4	..	2·8
Derby (mixed) - - - - -	33·6	3·5	...
Durham (mining) - - - -	21·6	13·	...
Lancaster (manufacturing) - - -	40·	20·	...
Leicester (do.) - - - -	34·1	...	14·
Monmouth (mining) - - - -	111·5	10·8	...
Northumberland (do.) - - -	29·1	1·	14·
Salop (mixed) - - - - - -	80·6	...	9·
Stafford (do.) - - - - -	39·5	27·2	...
Warwick (manufacturing) - - -	15·5	44·6	...
Worcester (mixed) - - - -	68·6	16·7	...
York (do.) - - - - -	54·6	25·3	...
Average of all England - - -	23·	13·4	...

It is true that, in the agricultural counties, ratios of excess nearly as high may be quoted, as for instance :—

	1840 to 1842.	1848.
Berks	22·8	31·6
Hereford . . .	68·7	30·4
Northampton . .	44·6	3·6
Sussex	35·8	24·
Westmoreland . .	53·8	

But these are isolated cases; the population of these counties being small, the additional offences indicated by these percentages, high as they are, was little more than one-third that of the additional offences in the county of Lancaster alone,—the actual increase for the five counties being 479 offences, and for Lancaster, 1417! A more striking mode of showing the intense action of seasons of *scarcity* and *dearness*, or of deficient employment on the manufacturing counties, is to place in juxtaposition the total additional crime in 1840 to 1842, as compared with 1836 to 1837, and the total population against the additional crime, in the five chief manufacturing counties, and the population of the same.

All England.

Total crime 1840 to 1842 av. 28,093 pop. 14,995,138
Ditto .   1836 ,, 1837 ,, 21,377 ,, 14,045,043

Increase . . 6,716

Five Manufacturing Counties.

TOTAL CRIME.	1836 to 1837.	1840 to 1842.	Population in 1841.
Cheshire - - -	568	1023	395,660
Lancashire - -	2579	3996	1,667,054
Stafford - - -	753	1156	510,504
Warwick - - -	788	1016	401,715
York - - - -	1282	2120	1,591,480
	5970	9311	4,566,413
		5970	
Increase - -	- -	3341	

Nearly *one-half* of the entire excess of crime in 1840 to 1842 was committed in five counties, containing about 30 *per cent.* of the population!

Striking as is the demonstration which these figures give, of the powerful action of periods of dear food and general distress, on the ratio of crime in the manufacturing districts, the demonstration admits of further emphasis. If individual years are contrasted,—say 1845 and 1842,—the former being a year of great commercial activity, of cheap food and general employment not often paralleled within the present century, and 1842 being the closing year of one of the most disastrous cycles in the history of the working classes—the demonstration is startling. The total of criminal offences of England and Wales in 1845 was 24,303 ; in 1842 it was 31,309 ; the excess of 1842 being 7006 offences, or about 29 per cent. In the five principal manufacturing counties the average excess, comparing the same year, was no less than 65 per cent., as under :—

COUNTIES.	Criminal Offences . 1845.	Criminal Offences 1842.	Excess 1842.	Percentage of Excess.
Chester - -	688	1086	398	58
Lancaster -	2852	4497	1645	58
Warwick -	769	1003	234	30
Stafford -	717	1485	768	107
York - -	1417	2598	1181	84
Total - -	6443	10,669	4226	65

The proof need not further be elaborated. It has been put thus strongly, and in so many forms, because the fact which it establishes, applied to the investigation of the comparative morality of the agricultural and manufacturing districts, or the progress and intensity of crime at particular periods, or the connexion of crime with ignorance, will throw a clear light on all these subjects, and dispose of a mountain of ill-assorted figures, and a host of false conclusions, which have been iterated, *usque ad nauseam*, by writers who either could not discover, or would not acknowledge THAT FACT. But more of this in the sequel.

It becomes an interesting subject of investigation, what kinds of criminal offences are most largely increased in periods of national distress, or whether *all* are affected in the same degree. The Table No. VI. affords the means of a general answer to the mooted points. It must be noted that the comparison in the Table, is betwixt the average of 1841, 1842, and 1843, and the average of 1844, 1845, and 1846. In the other Tables, the average of 1840 to 1842 has been taken. The reason why the one cycle is substituted for the other, is because of the stronger contrast afforded : 1841 to 1843 being a period of higher criminality than 1840 to 1842.

TABLE No. VI.

COUNTIES.	CLASS I. Serious Offences, including Malicious Offences against Property.*				CLASS II. Assaults.*				CLASS III. Offences against Property, with violence.*				CLASS IV. Simple Larcenies.*			
	Avrg. 1841 to 1843.	Avrg. 1844 to 1846.	Excs. 1841-3 over 1844-6	Excs. 1844-6 over 1841-3	Avrg. 1841 to 1843.	Avrg. 1844 to 1846.	Excs. 1841-3 over 1844-6	Excs. 1844-6 over 1841-3	Avrg. 1841 to 1843.	Avrg. 1844 to 1846.	Excs. 1841-3 over 1844-6	Excs. 1844-6 over 1841-3	Avrg. 1841 to 1843.	Avrg. 1844 to 1846.	Excs. 1841-3 over 1844-6	Excs. 1844-6 over 1841-3
Bedford	102	123		20	18	24		33	176	114	63		1057	836	26	
Berks	74	71	5		49	23	115		184	89	107		1153	945	22	
Bucks	78	100		27	2	31		1400	180	163	10		960	1014		5.5
Cambridge	60	133		120	24	36		50	114	115			870	899		3
Chester	146	94	55		48	26	90		181	101	80		1457	1056	39	
Cornwall	35	50		41	52	25	109		31	19	60		542	469	11	
Cumberland	33	60		80	28	16	75		22	44		100	440	424	4	
Derby	69	41	70		32	20	60		174	86	102		501	429	18	
Devon	47	69		50	15	14	7		51	58		15	883	880		
Dorset	68	82		20	23	38		56	108	54	100		937	747	28	
Durham	67	86		30	28	36		30	61	47	30		439	393	9	
Essex	89	117		30	29	25	13		180	145	25		1039	883	20	
Gloucester	93	95		4	60	34	80		146	104	41		1697	1290	31	
Hereford	79	78	1		26	34		31	260	199	30		1486	1042	43	
Hertford	63	92		46	25	18	41		132	104	27		1102	894	23	
Hunts	102	82	25		34	49		46	85	65	30		663	821		25

County																
Kent	78	75	...	...	43	40	...	7	125	91	30	...	1061	816	30	...
Lancaster	88	66	...	33	66	42	33	...	198	107	89	...	1149	842	36	...
Leicester	111	80	...	39	37	55	...	50	189	151	25	...	1314	1026	28	...
Lincoln	52	52	15	...	27	20	35	...	84	80	5	...	878	736	19	...
Middlesex	71	82	...	13	132	191	...	42	107	90	19	...	1263	1222	3	...
Monmouth	104	93	65	...	52	21	150	...	141	100	41	...	1240	1026	22	...
Norfolk	82	185	50	...	26	23	11	...	130	99	30	...	1172	1074	9	2
Northampton	60	91	38	...	30	27	10	...	110	81	35	...	855	872	...	...
Northumberland	44	60	...	...	36	22	65	...	92	60	53	...	544	407	34	...
Notts	56	56	25	5	20	22	...	10	100	76	32	...	940	450	109	...
Oxford	63	78	...	90	49	24	105	...	175	96	83	...	1344	1092	23	...
Rutland	94	90	...	7	79	13	500	...	188	135	40	...	705	677	4	...
Salop	104	56	...	15	83	23	49	...	145	61	133	...	1239	932	33	...
Somerset	92	86	...	70	82	64	29	...	211	162	30	9	1316	192	22	...
Southampton	84	73	...	...	53	24	115	...	90	98	...	...	1334	1108	19	...
Stafford	152	89	260	...	54	37	50	...	268	65	311	...	1344	916	47	...
Suffolk	44	153	15	...	25	12	108	...	132	124	6	...	1122	966	16	...
Surrey	65	75	...	...	53	56	...	...	108	77	40	...	848	764	11	...
Sussex	56	71	30	38	56	28	100	6	128	86	48	...	922	871	6	...
Warwick	77	57	...	...	17	34	...	100	251	152	66	...	1455	1078	35	...
Westmoreland	17	52	200	...	1	...	...	...	84	35	150	...	340	664	...	...
Wilts	85	86	...	...	27	57	...	40	127	82	55	...	1244	979	26	90
Worcester	137	115	...	19	60	49	40	...	218	247	...	14	1513	1314	15	...
York	57	53	...	8	19	18	5	...	160	88	80	...	741	468	58	...
All England	76	77	1	...	45	45	...	...	142	95	50	...	1004	873	22	...

* The Numbers given in these Columns show the number of Offences under each head, to 1,000,000 of the Population.

TABLE No. 6.—*Continued.*

COUNTIES.	CLASS V. All other Larcenies.*				CLASS VI. Embezzlements, Frauds.*				CLASS VII. Riots, Sedition, &c.*				CLASS VIII. All other Offences, chiefly against Property.*				Total of all Offences.*			
	Av. 1841 to 1843	Av. 1844 to 1846	Exs. 1841-3 over 1844-6	Exs. 1844-6 over 1841-3	Av. 1841 to 1843	Av. 1844 to 1846	Exs. 1841-3 over 1844-6	Exs. 1848-6 over 1841-3	Av. 1841 to 1843	Av. 1844 to 1846	Exs. 1841-3 over 1844-6	Exs. 1841-3 over 1841-3	Av. 1841 to 1843	Av. 1844 to 1846	Avrg. 1841-3 to 1844-6	Exs. 1844-6 over 1841-3	1841 to 1843.	1844 to 1846.	Ex. 1842 over 1845	Ex. 1845 over 1842
Bedford	194	211	...	9	111	79	40	...	148	88	70	...	115	97	15	...	1917	1850	23	...
Berks	160	142	16	...	152	95	60	...	99	77	28	...	117	78	50	...	1988	1820	37	...
Bucks	138	143	...	3	108	106	2	...	96	75	18	...	210	128	63	...	1772	1760	...	...
Cambridge	120	72	70	...	90	78	15	...	96	132	...	38	102	132	...	20	1476	1396	47	2
Chester	212	212	...	...	195	115	70	...	187	73	154	...	136	63	120	...	2563	1741	47	...
Cornwall	41	27	48	...	35	42	...	20	64	64	...	...	47	41	15	...	847	757	12	...
Cumberland	33	38	...	...	28	76	...	210	61	55	11	...	56	32	80	...	706	745	...	5
Derby	78	100	...	40	43	38	15	...	98	66	32	...	74	56	33	...	1079	836	28	...
Devon............	111	100	11	...	86	69	26	...	75	32	104	...	84	59	40	...	1354	1281	6	...
Dorset...........	34	87	...	157	136	76	80	...	34	16	112	...	108	81	35	...	1468	1181	24	...
Durham	54	36	50	...	67	52	30	...	40	86	...	115	60	30	100	...	906	766	5	...
Essex	366	248	48	...	130	89	45	...	58	33	76	...	103	83	25	...	2614	1623	24	...
Gloucester	321	353	...	10	125	148	...	19	49	47	4	...	311	159	95	...	2802	2230	25	...
Hereford.........	226	164	38	...	114	78	45	...	43	43	...	5	149	153	...	4	2383	1793	33	...
Hertford.........	226	196	15	...	100	72	39	...	75	49	50	...	207	128	70	...	1930	1548	25	...
Hunts	83	82	4	...	68	98	...	45	34	82	...	157	68	64	7	...	1139	1843	...	19

	C1	C2	C3	C4	C5	C6	C7	C8	C9	C10	C11	C12	C13	C14	C15	C16	C17	C18	C19	C20
Kent	627	232	6		95	75	26		76	34	120		122	78	55		1865	1467	27	
Lancaster	357	276	30		216	127	70		244	78	213		150	62	105		2438	1600	53	
Leicester	185	178	4	29	138	102	33		125	35	260		157	86	82	39	2256	1713	32	
Lincoln	43	55		19	78	75	4		57	30	90		67	92			1286	1140	13	
Middlesex	504	598			172	163			104	106		2	167	146	15		2520	2800		3
Monmouth	193	149	30		129	63	102		200	100	100		141	84	66		2200	1636	34	
Norfolk	122	118	3	5	104	118		11	55	23	140		113	104	8	34	1804	1694	6	
Northampton	100	105	5		130	55	138		220	46	380		75	108		6	1580	1385	14	
Northumberland	112	110	2	68	64	47	38		60	47	30		60	64		2	1012	817	24	
Notts	72	119			56	26	119		100	26	65		68	69	94		1412	844	43	
Oxford	196	32	50		196	108	81		126	72	80		140	72	372		2289	1674	37	
Rutland	141	90	55		141	13	900		94	135		46	141	32	7		1583	1185	34	
Salop	136	92	48		115	72	60		108	12	800		86	80	29		1966	1328	48	
Somerset	192	158	22	9	162	128	26		163	101	62		178	139	60		2414	1930	25	
Southampton	77	62	25		100	71	40		106	49	120		95	58	202		1921	1543	24	
Stafford	133	144			106	83	29		276	67	311		130	49			2483	1450	71	
Suffolk	106	91	16		115	94	23		50	55		10	62	78		40	1656	1578	5	
Surrey	254	273		27	116	83	40		58	41	40		97	142		48	1599	149	7	
Sus-ex	214	274			131	132			75	90		20	131	84	80		1733	1636	6	
Warwick	357	266	36		132	116	15		67	75		12	191	106	80		2547	1884	35	36
Westmoreland	52	19	175		34	34			68	52	30		34	5	380		634	861		
Wilts	166	150	10	21	115	90	28		81	45	80		115	85	35		1960	1554	26	
Worcester	261	316			124	94	33		145	69	110		171	122	40		2629	2326	13	
York	154	111	39		77	46	70		108	44	148		98	53	88		1414	881	66	
All England	235	212	11		116	94	24		115	61	90		130	87	50		1·23	1644	24	

* The Numbers given in these Columns show the number of Offences, under each head, to 1,000,000 of the Population.

The numbers given in each column express the proportions of each class of crime to each million of the population ; and being placed in parallel columns, the action of dear food, and deficient employment, in each of the eight classes of crime, is perceived at a glance, for the whole of England, and separately for each county. It will greatly assist the judgment, if, in addition to the juxtaposition of these percentages, the total average number of offences under each class are also placed in juxtaposition. The inspection of the former shows simply the relative proportions of two things : the inspection of the latter gives their absolute bulk and dimensions.

Abstract of the Criminal Offences in England in the under-mentioned Periods, showing the Total Number of Offences in each Class, and the Excess or Deficiency in each Class, comparing 1844 *to* 1846, *with* 1841 *to* 1843.

	Criminal Offences.				Percentage.	
CLASS OF OFFENCES.	1841 to 1843.	Centesimal Proportions.	1844 to 1846.	Centesimal Proportions.	Excess 1844 to 1846 over 1841 to 1843.	Excess 1841 to 1843 over 1844 to 1846.
No. 1. Serious Offences -	1151	4·	1236	5·1	·7	..
„ 2. Assaults - - -	688	2·5	769	2·9	12	..
„ 3. Offences against Property, with Violence - -	2145	7·5	1520	6·1	..	41
„ 4. Simple Larcenies -	15,967	54·9	13,853	56·4	..	15
„ 5. All other Larcenies	3373	12·3	3366	13·8	..	
„ 6. Embezzlements, Frauds, &c. -	1781	6·	1497	6.	..	19
„ 7. Riots, Sedition, &c.	1738	6·	981	4·	..	77
„ 8. All other Offences chiefly against Property - -	1999	6·8	1397	5·7	..	43
Total - - -	28,842	100	24,619	100	..	17

In this Table, the last column requires adjustment to the population. This being done, the excess of each class of offences in the respective periods, would be as follows :—

CLASS OF OFFENCES.	Excess 1844 to 1846 over 1841 to 1843. Percentage.	Excess 1841 to 1843 over 1844 to 1846. Percentage.
No. 1 Class - - - -	1	...
„ 2 „ - - - - -	Par	Par
„ 3 „ - - - - -	...	50
„ 4 „ - - - - -	...	21
„ 5 „ - - - - -	7	...
„ 6 „ - - - - -	...	25
„ 7 „ - - - - -	...	90
„ 8 „ - - - - -	...	50
All Offences - -	...	25

It appears from these two Tables, that periods of distress do not aggravate the causes, whatever they may be, which lead to the fouler and more atrocious offences against the person ; nor yet does it appear that personal quarrels, mere assaults, are increased by them. * Nor is the increase of simple theft at all remarkable, being under the average increase of *all* crime. It is far different with all classes of offences, in which practised skill and daring, and systematic fraud, are more or less concerned, separately or conjointly. Burglaries, highway robberies, house and shop breaking, receiving stolen goods, frauds, forgery and uttering base coin, are fearfully augmented. It would seem as if the

* The assaults on police officers are placed under the class, Riots, Sedition, &c.

number, activity, and recklessness of the adult classes of
the criminal population was greatly increased by the action
of general distress; a fact painfully suggestive of the
mode in which past periods of deep national calamity,
attributable to an unwise and unjust national policy, have
inflicted great moral evils, as well as great social wrongs,
and domestic and personal sufferings.   But it is ever so—
a political injustice is only another name for a moral evil.

One other class of offences remains to be noticed,—
Riot, Sedition, &c. Not more surely does a period of general
distress directly increase the more serious offences against
property, than it indirectly leads to that class of offences which
affects the peace of the body, social and political.   Forced
idleness, with want urging on one side and strong passions
and resentments perhaps, on the other, is a bad conser-
vator of order.   Hence discontent, the imputation of felt
evils to social arrangement or to particular classes of the
community, or to their special and peculiar privileges ; and
as the inevitable sequence — sedition and breaches of
the peace.   Not that all such discontent is unjustifiable,
or that all such imputations are erroneous, either in whole
or part ; but discontent engenders disaffection and insubordination, when the gnawings of hunger are felt ; and
hungry men are neither very cool in their reasonings, nor
very logical in their conclusions.

The excess in this class of offences, comparing 1841 to
1843, with 1844 to 1846, is 90 per cent.   It will be shown
presently, in what particular counties the excess took
place.   The final cause of the excess,—the great distress
pervading nearly all the manufacturing districts, pro-
ducing heartburnings, discontent, tumults, and an extensive, outbreak familiarly known as the "plug strike" of

1842,—is matter of history. The respective totals of offences under the several heads of Riots, Sedition, Assaults on Police Officers, &c., for the periods compared, were 1738, or the average of 1841 to 1843, and 981 on the average of 1844 to 1846 ; but if the latter number be reduced, *pro rata*, to the increase of population, the respective numbers would be about 1738 and 910, leaving an excess of 838, as the incidence of seasons of privation and suffering amongst the people, as regards this class of offences. As in round numbers, the difference in the totals of all offences for the periods compared, was 6000 (the actual numbers in 1844 to 1846 being adjusted to the population at that time), it appears that nearly one-seventh of this increase consists of acts of insubordination and resistance to civil authority.

Probably the whole extent to which all crime is affected, and the precise proportions in which particular classes are affected by the pressure of general distress, will be most clearly exhibited by the following tabular view, in in which the respective ratios are given, and the ratio of excess is stated in millionth parts ; in other words, the numbers in the first and second columns show how many offences of each class there were in the respective periods, in *each million of the population*, as in Table VI.

CLASS OF OFFENCES.	1841 to 1843.	1844 to 1846.	Percentage excess 1844 to 1846 over 1841 to 1843.	Percentage excess 1841 to 1843 over 1844 to 1846.
No. 1. Serious Offences -	76	77	1	...
,, 2. Assaults - - -	45	45	Par	Par
,, 3. Offences against Property, with Violence - - -	142	95	...	50
,, 4. Simple Larcenies	1064	873	...	21
,, 5. All other Larcenies	226	212	...	7
,, 6. Embezzlements, Frauds, &c. -	118	94	...	25
,, 7. Riots, Sedition, &c.	115	61	...	90
,, 8. All other Offences	133	88	...	50
Total - -	1919	1545	...	25

Influence of Variations in the Price of Food on Crime, in the several Counties of England.

IT would require details quite unsuitable for a pamphlet, to set forth the exact proportions of crime under each of the 8 Classes, and also to place the several counties in the order of criminality under each Class. The Table, therefore, only sets forth the former particulars; but the omission of the latter can be partially supplied by occasional reference to the Table No. VI., in the course of the remarks which will be offered upon it.

Class 1.—*Serious Offences,*

For the whole of England, 1841 to 1843, exhibit a less amount of this class of offences, than 1844 to 1846 ; yet in 17 counties there was an excess varying from 5 to 90 per cent. in the former than the latter period. The highest excess was in :—

Shropshire . . . . 90 per cent.
Derby . . . . 70 ,,
Stafford . . . . 70 ,,
Chester . . . . 55 ,,
Leicester . . . . 39 ,,
Warwick . . . . 38 ,,
Lancaster . . . . . . 33 ,,

It has been shown in a previous page, that the total number of the serious offences in 1841 to 1843, was 1151 ; and in 1844 to 1846, 1236—the difference being 81.   Now, in the 17 counties alluded to, the number of such offences committed in the former period, exceeded those of the latter by 140.   It is evident, therefore, that in the remaining 23 counties, the proportion of such offences must have been considerably greater in the period 1844 to 1846, than in the period 1841 to 1843.   The extraordinary phenomenon is presented of a much higher ratio of serious offences in the year of prosperity in almost all the agricultural counties, and a very greatly diminished ratio in the manufacturing counties.   It may be, that to judge correctly of the ratio of the serious offences, the comparison should extend over a larger cycle of years—the causes of such crime not being of constant and uniform intensity, and their amount too, being happily not so large in any particular county, but that the addition in any given year, of a very small number, greatly affects the ratio for that year compared with others. The comparison of 1841 to 1843 with 1844 to 1846, as to this class of offences, furnishes no indications that variations in the price of food exercise any influence, either in augmenting or diminishing the total ratio for the entire kingdom.

Class 2.—Assaults.

The same remark applies to the Second Class; indeed, so variable seem to be the impulses which lead to them, that the 3rd column, under this head, exhibits every graduation of difference from 5 to 1400 per cent.

Class 3.—Offences against Property, with Violence.

Under this head, the evidence of a disturbing action in the dear period, is quite decisive. Only 4 counties show a lower ratio of such offences in 1841 to 1843, than in 1844 to 1846. The average excess for all England in the former period was 50 per cent. Excluding the small county of Westmoreland, the counties in which the excess exceeds that average, are the following :—

	Per cent.		Per cent.
Stafford	311	York	80
Salop	133	Chester	80
Berks	107	Warwick	66
Derby	102	Bedford	63
Dorset	100	Cornwall	60
Lancaster	89	Wilts	55
Oxford	83	Northumberland	53.

All the great seats of manufactures are included in this enumeration ; and although the ratio of violent offences against property was also higher in the agricultural counties, the excess is, in nearly all, below the general average. The element of disturbance, in whatever manner it may operate, pervades nearly the whole kingdom; but with a far more active force in the manufacturing, than in the rural counties.

Class 4.—Simple Larcenies.

In this Class again, the manufacturing counties exhibit the highest ratios of excess. The average excess for all England is 22 per cent., and the counties exceeding that are :—

	Per cent.		Per cent.
Notts . . .	109	Shropshire. .	33
York . . .	58	Gloucester . .	31
Stafford . .	47	Kent . . .	30
Hereford . .	43	Dorset . . .	28
Chester . .	39	Leicester . .	28
Lancaster . .	36	Bedford . .	26
Warwick . .	35	Wilts . . .	26
Northumberland	34		

In this list, the 5 leading manufacturing counties of Cheshire, Lancashire, Staffordshire, Warwickshire, and Yorkshire, all appear, and are greatly above the average, as under the preceding class; the only county that can rank as essentially an agricultural one, is the county of Dorset.

Class 5.—All other Larcenies.

- The Fifth Class, ALL OTHER LARCENIES, though it contains evidence of the same influence as the preceding classes, does not require minute remark. The Class comprises larceny to the value of £5 in dwelling-houses; larceny from the person, and larceny by servants:

the aggregate constituting in 1842, 12·3, and in 1845, 13·8 centesimal parts of the total of crime. It is quite obvious, that crime of this Class will be most rife in the more densely peopled and wealthy counties, as will appear on reference to the Table, where Middlesex, Gloucester, Worcester, Lancaster, Sussex, Warwick, Surrey, Kent, and Essex, rank respectively in millionth parts, at 598, 353, 316, 276, 274, 266, 253, 252 and 248, in the year 1845, the average of all England being only 212. It does not appear that any very definite conclusion can be drawn from the comparison of the two periods, on the point mooted in this chapter.

Class 6.—Embezzlements, Frauds, Receiving Stolen Goods, &c.

The excess in this Class of offences in the year of distress is 24 per cent. on all England,—and the excess is common to all the counties except five—Cornwall, Cumberland, Huntingdon, Gloucester, and Norfolk. It is obvious, from the nature of the offences, that Cornwall, Huntingdon, and Cumberland, in which the general ratio is low, will be little affected by changes in the material condition of the people, or in the activity of trade and commerce;—and in Gloucester and Norfolk, the smaller amount of this class of offences in the periods of depression cannot affect the proof which the remaining 35 counties afford, that such periods greatly increase the number. The range in the variations of the ratios of these 35 counties is exceedingly wide, viz.—from 2 per cent. to 138 (including Rutland, in which the large variation of 900 per cent. is questionably attributable to some accidental circumstances), and this wide range is common alike to the

agricultural and the manufacturing counties. No safe
inference could be drawn from the Table, that the one, or
the other Class, was more affected by periods of distress.

Class 7.—Riots, Sedition, &c.

This Class presents the highest ratio of increase or excess
of crime,—90 per cent. The exceptions are quite unimportant. Middlesex is never much affected by vicissitudes
in trade or variations in the price of food. Its population
may be less actively engaged in times of depression ; but
so vast a proportion of its inhabitants are beyond the reach
of such conditions of trade, that it may be disregarded in
the investigation. Warwick, another exception, ought to
be associated with Stafford and Worcester, in order to come
to a correct conclusion. Birmingham contains nearly one
half the population of the county, and, like London, is
under strict municipal rule. The remainder of the county,
excepting Coventry, is chiefly rural and agricultural. Birmingham, in fact, is essentially an integral industrial part
of Staffordshire and Worcestershire, and it is by the effect
produced on those two counties by changes in the state of
trade, that the influence of such circumstances on Birmingham must be tested. Huntingdon and Rutland may be
left out of consideration altogether, and there remain then
only Cambridge, Hereford, Suffolk, and Sussex, as exceptions. As exceptions they are unimportant ; the average
excess of all England in 1842 being 90 ; whilst these
counties show respectively, an excess in 1845 of 38,
5, 10, and 20. The counties exhibiting the most powerful action of distress in the class of offences, are the
following :—

	Percentage. Excess in 1842.		Percentage. Excess in 1842.
Shropshire . .	800	Norfolk . .	140
Northampton .	380	Kent . . .	120
Stafford . .	311	Southampton	120
Leicester . .	260	Dorset . .	112
Lancaster . .	213	Worcester .	110
Chester . . .	154	Devon . .	104
York	148	Monmouth .	100

It has been shown (page 63) that the totals of this class of crime for 1842 and 1845, were respectively, 1738 and 910, leaving an excess of 757 against the former period. Of this excess, the 14 counties enumerated furnished 690; of which 505 was supplied by the 4 manufacturing counties of Chester, Lancaster, Stafford, and York,—being 66 per cent. of the entire excess of 1842. The inference from this fact needs no elaboration.

Class 8.—*All other other Offences, chiefly against Property.*

This Class is miscellaneous—including cattle, horse and sheep stealing, stealing shrubs, stealing goods in process of manufacture, forgery, deer and fish stealing. It would be a tedious, and perhaps unprofitable task, to eliminate the exact increase or decrease in the respective periods, of each of these subdivisions of offences. It is sufficiently clear, that, excluding the two small counties of Rutland and Westmoreland, for reasons already given, the manufacturing districts show, not merely the largest ratio of excess in 1842, but a very preponderating one. The excess in all England being 50 per cent., the following manufacturing counties exhibit a much higher ratio :—

Stafford . . . . 202 per cent.

Lancaster . . . . . . 140 „

Chester . . . . 120 . „

York . . . . 88 „

Leicester . . . . . . 82 „

Warwick . . . . . . 80 „

The only other counties approaching this excess are Gloucester, 95 ; Durham, 100 ; and Sussex, 80. The first is, in a great measure, a manufacturing county ; and the second largely engaged in mining. The only agricultural counties which present a high average, are Cumberland, 80 ; Sussex, 80 ; and Bucks, 63.

The influence of variations in the price of food (or in other words, of general prosperity on the one hand, and general distress on the other), on the ratio of crime, has now been tested by a careful analysis of eight distinct classes of offences. The specific object of the analysis was to discover, if possible, whether there was any difference, and what difference, in the effect of such periods, on counties of distinct and different industrial and social organization. The results of the analysis may now be stated.

It is necessary, however, to clear away extraneous matter. Under each class of offences, very varying ratios of excess are exhibited, sometimes inclining to the period of prosperity, and at others to the period of depression. On a careful reference to the Table, it will be evident that most of the extreme divergencies from what appears on the face of the Tables to be a general rule, occur in counties of small population, and of peculiar social organization. Comparison, to be of any value, must be betwixt counties which

are distinctly different in organization, if the object be to
ascertain the influence of particular organizations. It
would answer no good purpose to include such counties as
Rutland, Westmoreland, or Huntingdonshire, in any comparison, having either of these objects in view; because
the scale of comparison is too confined, and the proportions
of offences are liable to be disturbed by mere accidents (so
to speak) in the number of offences for particular years.
In the following summary, therefore, the indications of
change afforded by these counties are disregarded.

The first, second, and fifth Classes, viz., Serious Offences,
Assaults, and all other Larcenies (that is, all larcenies
separate from simple larcenies), afford no decisive indication of more intense action of periods of dear food on
the one than the other section of the counties. It must,
however, be understood, that no absolute conclusion is
affirmed on this point. One comparison cannot be considered as decisive with respect to classes of offences, not
large in number relatively to all offences, and, as respects
which, the one comparison made, shows no important
ratio of difference.

The third, fourth, sixth, seventh, and eighth Classes, on
the contrary, give unmistakeable indications that seasons
of distress greatly increase crime.

It may be necessary to recall the reader's attention to
the proof afforded (in page 51), that whether 1842 be compared with 1845, or 1836,—or 1848 with 1845, the same
result stands out in strong relief; namely, that periods of
dear food and commercial depression are periods of increasing crime. It is desirable to obviate here the possible cavil
that the comparison is confined to two periods only. It
can be proved, if needful, that 1836, compared with 1842,

or 1848 compared with 1845, would establish the same conclusions, as will now be presented as the results of a comparison of 1845 with 1842.

Putting in this *caveat* against objection on the ground of a narrow investigation of facts, perhaps the best mode of exhibiting the action of seasons of distress on these five classes of crime in different classes of counties, will be to place in juxtaposition the proportions of such crimes in five of the manufacturing and five of the agricultural counties, and to indicate the percentage of that action.

E

CLASS 3. OFFENCES AGAINST PROPERTY, *accompanied
with Violence.*

5. *Manufacturing Counties.*

COUNTY.	Ratio in Parts of One Million. 1842.	Ratio in Parts of One Million. 1845.	Excess, 1842.	Excess, 1845.
Chester - - - -	181	101	80	...
Lancaster - - -	198	107	89	...
Stafford - - - -	268	65	311	...
Warwick - - -	251	152	66	...
York - - - -	160	88	80	...
All England - -	142	95	50	...

CLASS 4. SIMPLE LARCENIES.

Chester - - - -	1457	1056	39	...
Lancaster - - -	1149	842	36	...
Stafford - - - -	1344	916	47	...
Warwick - - -	1455	1078	35	...
York - - - -	741	468	58	...
All England - -	1064	873	22	...

CLASS 6. EMBEZZLEMENTS, FRAUDS, &c.

Chester - - - -	195	115	70	...
Lancaster - - -	216	127	70	...
Stafford - - - -	106	83	29	...
Warwick - - -	132	116	15	...
York - - - -	77	46	70	...
All England - -	116	94	24	...

CLASS 3. OFFENCES AGAINST PROPERTY, *accompanied
with Violence.*

5. *Agricultural Counties.*

COUNTY.	Ratio in Parts of One Million. 1842.	Ratio in Parts of One Million. 1845.	Excess, 1842.	Excess, 1845.
Devon - - - -	51	58	...	15
Lincoln - - - -	84	80	5	...
Norfolk - - - -	130	99	30	...
Suffolk - - - -	132	124	6	...
Somerset - - -	211	162	30	...
... ...	...	...	...	...

CLASS 4. SIMPLE LARCENIES.

Devon - - - -	883	880	...	...
Lincoln - - - -	878	736	19	...
Norfolk - - - -	1172	1074	9	...
Suffolk - - - -	1122	966	16	...
Somerset - - -	1334	1092	22	...
... ...	...	...	...	...

CLASS 6. EMBEZZLEMENTS, FRAUDS, &c.

Devon - - - -	88	69	26	...
Lincoln - - - -	78	75	4	...
Norfolk - - - -	104	118	...	11
Suffolk - - - -	115	94	23	...
Somerset - - -	162	128	26	...
... ...	...	...	...	...

CLASS 7. RIOT, SEDITION, &c.

5. *Manufacturing Counties.*

COUNTY.	Ratio in Parts of One Million. 1842.	Ratio in Parts of One Million. 1845.	Excess, 1842.	Excess, 1845.
Chester - - - -	187	73	154	...
Lancaster - - -	244	78	213	...
Stafford - - - -	276	67	311	...
Warwick - - -	67	75	...	12
York - - -	108	44	148	...
All England - -	115	61	90	...

CLASS 8. ALL OTHER OFFENCES.

Chester - - - -	136	62	120	...
Lancaster - - -	150	62	140	...
Stafford - - -	150	49	202	...
Warwick - - -	191	106	80	...
York - - -	98	53	88	...
All England - -	130	87	50	...

TOTAL OF CRIME.

Chester - - - -	2562	1741	47	...
Lancaster - - -	2458	1600	53	...
Stafford - - - -	2183	1450	71	...
Warwick - - -	2547	1884	35	...
York - - - -	1414	881	66	...
All England - -	1923	1544	24	...

RIOT, SEDITION, &c.

5. *Agricultural Counties.*

COUNTY.	Ratio in Parts of One Million. 1842.	Ratio in Parts of One Million. 1845.	Excess, 1842.	Excess, 1845.
Devon - - - -	75	32	104	...
Lincoln - - - -	57	30	90	...
Norfolk - - - -	55	23	140	...
Suffolk - - - -	50	55	...	10
Somerset - - -	163	101	62	...
... ...	...	...	...	...

CLASS 8. ALL OTHER OFFENCES.

COUNTY.	Ratio in Parts of One Million. 1842.	Ratio in Parts of One Million. 1845.	Excess, 1842.	Excess, 1845.
Devon - - - -	84	59	40	...
Lincoln - - - -	67	92	...	39
Norfolk - - - -	113	104	8	...
Suffolk - - - -	62	78	...	40
Somerset - - -	178	139	...	...
... ...	...	...	...	...

TOTAL OF CRIME.

COUNTY.	Ratio in Parts of One Million. 1842.	Ratio in Parts of One Million. 1845.	Excess, 1842.	Excess, 1845.
Devon - - - -	1354	1281	6	...
Lincoln - - - -	1286	1140	13	...
Norfolk - - - -	1804	1694	6	...
Suffolk - - - -	1656	1578	5	...
Somerset - - -	2414	1930	25	...
... ...	...	...	...	...

It is impossible to mistake the indications of these figures. Not only is the action of the circumstances under review most distinctly shown, but the very violent character of that action on the ·manufacturing counties is also proved. The contrast may be made even more striking by placing in juxtaposition the average ratio of crime to population in the two years 1836 and 1845, in five manufacturing and five agricultural counties respectively, as compared with 1841. The relation of the middle column to the other two is unmistakeable.

5. *Manufacturing Counties.*

COUNTY.	1836.	1841.	1845.
	Crime, 1 in	Crime, 1 in	Crime, 1 in
Chester - - -	568	387	744
Lancaster - - -	582	417	621
Stafford - - -	614	441	687
Warwick - - -	468	405	529
York - - - -	1155	750	1088

5. *Agricultural Counties.*

COUNTY.	1836.	1841.	1845.
	Crime, 1 in	Crime, 1 in	Crime, 1 in
Devon - - - -	898	755	766
Lincoln - - -	845	859	851
Norfolk - - -	689	570	589
Suffolk - - -	624	634	638
Somerset - - -	502	400	516

It is quite obvious that any comparison betwixt counties so differently affected by variations in the *price of food*, and the state of trade, which exclude, or disregard, the influence of these variations, can only lead to error.

Nor must it be omitted to notice, that whilst four out of the five manufacturing counties show a much smaller ratio of crime in 1845 than 1836, the proportions of crime for the same year are greatly increased in two of the agricultural counties, and very slightly diminished in the *three* other counties.

THE COMPARATIVE MORALITY OF THE MANUFACTURING AND THE AGRICULTURAL COUNTIES.

THE point mooted in this chapter is one which has been disputed with much warmth. There is a necessity, therefore, to approach it with the greater calmness and good temper. It cannot be a matter *unimportant* to this country, whether its manufacturing system is improving or deteriorating the character of its population; and the question is of the more moment, because it may be, that whatever of evil at present stands connected with the manufacturing and factory system, is not essential to it, and may admit of cure. Nay, it may be possible,—and the idea is not shirked,—that the manufacturing system may contain in it elements of intellectual and moral progress which do not belong to the agricultural.

It may be laid down, then, as a principle, that all comparison of comparative morality must have reference to periods which are alike in their social circumstances. Now it has been proved that seasons of dear food, far more powerfully affect the ratio of crime in the manufacturing than in the agricultural counties. It is obvious, that it is, at least, only to blink the consideration of a difficulty, to neglect this difference in the intensity of action betwixt the two classes of counties; and the more especially as it is quite evident, on the very face of the comparison, that the specific action of periods of distress does not impede

A

the onward progress of certain moral causes which are at work in the manufacturing counties, and which are decisively indicated by the re-action in the amount of crime already noticed, when those periods have passed.

But the *rationale* of that more intense action may be demanded. It is not difficult to make out.

Whatever the price of food may be, always excepting prolonged periods, the number of persons employed in agriculture is not greatly affected. *Real wages* are, no doubt, affected ; but still, there is not much difference in the efficient *demand for labour*. It is far otherwise with the demand for labour in the manufacturing districts,—or, more properly speaking, *it was*,—for what the influence of seasons of dear food, or rather, of variations in the home supply of food may be, on the ratio of wages, and the condition of the people, under the system of free trade, remains to be seen.

. An advance in the price of food affects the demand for manufacturing labour, through its action on the demand for the commodities on which that labour is employed. The great consumers are the middle and operative classes. The most important item of expenditure with the entire of the latter class, and a considerable portion of the former, is that on *food*. It is obvious, that, as the outlay on food increases, the outlay on something else must be diminished ; and whether the saving be effected by a less consumption of home-made goods, or colonial produce, or foreign commodities, the result is the same as regards the production of manufactures, and the employment of labour. If there be a less consumption of home manufactures, the action on labour is direct and immediate,—if of colonial or foreign produce, the action is indirect and somewhat

E 3

remote—but not the less sure. The exports ultimately depend on the ability to consume colonial and foreign productions.

But the lessened consumption of home manufactures, necessarily following a rise in the price of food, brings with it far worse evils than the immediate and direct reduction in the amount of employment. A lessened demand for any article is synonymous with a lower price for it, and a lower price leads to caution on the part of all persons connected with the trade in it, either as dealers in the raw material, or fabricators of goods, of which the raw material constitutes the whole or part. The weaker class of dealers is affected by the fall in price; and if the depression continues, failures increase—general credit is damaged—monetary accommodation is contracted; and thus, by a cumulative process, the final effect of a rise in the price of food, on the employment of manufacturing labour, is twice or threefold in amount that which would seem commensurate with the mere falling off in the ability to pay for manufactured articles; and the longer food remains high in price, and the more aggravated are its evil effects, in the mode described. The period of bad harvests, from 1838 to 1842, was an instance of this cumulative action of a protracted period of dear food. The action of the directly opposite case, viz.—of a low price of food, and especially if continuous, establishes the principle enunciated. With the good harvest of 1842, the tide of employment, which had been ebbing since 1838, turned; and it continued to flow until the potato blight of 1846. Again, since the enactment of Sir Robert Peel's measures of free trade, and the consequent fall in price of all kinds of food, employment has overtaken the supply of labour, and general activity and prosperity mark every department of trade and manufactures. It would be a waste of argument to show that the operation of a low price of food on employment,—on wages,— on the prices of manufactured goods,— on exports, and on general mercantile credit, is exactly the converse of the action of a high price. The one set of phenomena is to the other, just what health and sickness are, as the results of sufficient, or insufficient aliment, to sustain the wear and tear of the body, only the action is in the one case positive, in the other negative.

The demonstration of the intense action of periods of distress in augmenting crime generally, and its special intensity in augmenting crime in the manufacturing districts, is too complete and palpable to be met any longer by the flippant iteration of the cuckoo note, " that poverty does not increase criminal offences." The immediate cause of such crimes as come before the quarter sessions and the assizes may not be poverty, probably just because the crimes may be, in few, if any cases, the *first* which the criminals have committed. The fact remains, and it is undeniable, that in periods of general distress and destitution, crimes of all kinds, except the more serious offences against the person, and simple assaults, are increased 24 per cent. on the average of all England, and on the average of the five principal manufacturing districts, 51 per cent. ; that crimes against property, accompanied with *violence*, are increased 50 per cent. on the average of all England, and 103 per cent. on the average of the five counties named ; and that breaches of the peace, sedition, &c., are increased 90 per cent. on the average of all· England, and 164 per cent. on the average of the five manufacturing counties.

The process by which such disastrous effects are produced, in periods of privation and suffering, is not so easy

of elimination, as is the fact itself; but it may not be rash
to venture upon some speculation of the *modus operandi*.

The fact may safely be assumed, that there is at, all
times, in every country advanced in civilization, a large
class of persons, bordering, as to pecuniary circumstances,
on absolute destitution, and, as to morality, on the verge
of open outrage of the laws, governmental or moral, which
that country acknowledges. It is to deny the experience
of all past and all existing nations, to affirm the contrary.
Nor is it much less a repudiation of all experience to assert,
that any degree of wisdom in the management of human
affairs, or in the appliance of moral means, which is con-
ceivable, as a practicable, realizable thing, will ever entirely
eradicate the class in question. The most Utopian inspector
of Government Schools would hardly venture to assert
the possibility of attaining to such a condition of society,
and still less, the probability of its early consummation.
Even in seasons of general prosperity, there are but too
many in the social and moral condition indicated. That
condition may be accurately described in one short sen-
tence, as an imminent exposure to the temptations which
always accompany destitution and idleness, and a moral
power of resistance which is all but *nil*. The class so
situated, is but too large a one at all times; but in periods
of great depression in trade, and consequent suffering
amongst the operative classes, it is rapidly augmented in
number by the less educated and less morally disciplined,
who cannot stand the fiery ordeal of protracted idleness,
and its inevitable concomitant, protracted temptation. The
longer the period of commercial prostration, the more
active are the elements of evil. Day by day, the criminal
class is augmented, and day after day stereotypes in bolder

relief every phase and characteristic of the moral evil which is at work. The occasional act becomes a constant habit; principle is overlaid, and conscience drugged and stupified. And whilst the direct incentives to evil conduct are daily multiplied in number and aggravated in force, all the sweet persuasives to virtuous conduct are neutralized, or else, contrariwise, rouse only feelings of *anger or desperation.* Thus house, wife, family, are regarded with bitterness; bitterness brings discontent, and discontent ends in a malignant feeling towards all that is happier than itself. Nor does the return to prosperity obliterate the evil which a long cycle of distress has produced. Work may be resumed, and the former comforts gladden the household, but the *trail and slime* of the moral evil which has dwelt in the heart and ruled there, remains, and will evidence itself in a thousand forms. Self-respect has been seriously damaged, the sentiments have become polluted, the restraints on vicious or dishonest conduct weakened,—the whole man is morally degraded, and, in the majority of cases, the former standard is never regained. Nor can it admit of a doubt, that many, very many, are thrown off in every period of severe distress, from the ranks of the industrious and virtuous, who never return to them, but enter upon a career of vicious indulgence, fed by marauding on the rest of society, which terminates in the penal colony, or in a death of misery and horror!

Enough has been said to show the absolute necessity, in order to a fair comparison of the morality of the manufacturing with the agricultural counties, of instituting such comparison only betwixt the ratios of crime in each group, in periods of steady trade and good employment. But there are yet two other elements demanding consideration, and the action of which on the absolute ratio of crime in each group must be estimated before any safe conclusion can be drawn : these are the influence of age on crime, and the proportion of the operative class, and especially the *mere labourers,* to all other classes.

Mr. Neison has shown, in an elaborate paper in the Statistical Magazine for October 1846, that about 64 per cent. of all criminal offences in England and Wales is committed by persons from 15 to 30 years of age. The inference has somewhat hastily been drawn, that, as the proportion of persons at such ages in the manufacturing districts is considerably greater than in the agricultural, crime is *proportionably* enhanced in the former. The fact is notorious enough, that immigration takes place *into* the manufacturing counties, *from* the-agricultural, principally at an early age : the bulk of the immigrants being probably betwixt 15 and 25 years of age. But the conclusion, from the preponderance of persons betwixt those ages in the manufacturing counties, that crime is increased thereby, that is, *in its absolute ratio to the entire population,* is not correct. The simple solution of what appears to be a gross contradiction is this :—That, in a population comprising an excess of persons betwixt 15 and 30, the proportion of persons under twenty is also in excess. Now the latter section is obviously the least criminal. It is quite true that the criminality of the population above 30 years of age is considerably less than that of the population from 20 to 30 years of age ; and, therefore, as the more adult class in the manufacturing districts forms a smaller section relatively to the entire population, than in the agricultural, there is, so far, a drawback against the excess of the *less* criminal population,—the juvenile, in the former

counties. The effect of these several variations in the
proportion of the ages, is such as almost to neutralize each
other: so that, after all, the absolute ratio of crime in any
county may be taken as the exact index of its crime, when
its population is reduced to the average proportions of all
England. A few figures will make this plain.

	Aged under 20 years, per cent.	Aged 20 to 25, per cent.	Aged 25 to 30, per cent.	Aged 30 and upwards per cent.
Proportion of persons in all England -	45·8	9·7	8·0	36·5
Criminals in same, 1 in	971	262	363	753

Total criminality, 1 in 641.

It needs only a glance to perceive, that if in any given
county, the population 20 years of age and under, are in
excess, as well as the population 20 to 30 years of age, that a
small excess of the former section will neutralize a great
excess in the latter section. A case or two will make this
clear. Here are three counties placed in juxtaposition, with
the most diverse proportions at the several ages, but an
equal ratio of crime on the average of all ages; and yet,
on assimilating the ratios of the ages in all three, the
average ratio of crime is almost undisturbed.

COUNTY.	POPULATION.				Ratio of crime, 1 in
	Under 20 years of age, per cent.	20 to 25 years, per cent.	25 to 30 years, per cent.	30 and upwards per cent.	
Berks -	45·7	9·2	7·6	37·5	634
Lancaster-	47·0	10·4	7·7	33·9	621
Suffolk -	47·2	9·0	7·2	36·6	638

The ratios of the population at each section of age being adjusted according to the ratios of *all England*, and the total amount of crime being calculated on that adjustment, the absolute ratios come out as follows:—

Berkshire - - - - - 1 in 627
Lancaster - - - - - 1 ,, 628
Suffolk - - - - - - 1 ,, 625   .

The *rationale* is quite evident. An excess of the population at the *most criminal age*, is almost invariably accompanied by an excess of the population at *the least criminal age*, and the excess of crime at the one age is neutralized by the paucity of crime at the other;—the difference in the proportions of the population, upwards of 30 years of age, having no perceptible influence in modifying the effect. This will be best shown by placing in connexion the ratios of crime, at each age, in the three counties named.

COUNTY.	CRIME.			
	Under 20 years of age, 1 in	20 to 25 years of age, 1 in	25 to 30 years of age, 1 in	30 years of age and upwards, 1 in
Berks - -	916	221	336	819
Lancaster -	973	281	352	664
Suffolk -	851	218	292	1030

Here is a palpable excess of criminality in the agricultural counties of Berks and Suffolk, at the juvenile age, and also up to the age of 30 years,—neutralized, however, by an excess of criminality in the manufacturing county of Lancaster, in the population *above 30 years of age*.

It is quite evident, that, comparing county with county, or agricultural with manufacturing counties, it is entirely

fallacious to take general averages. Such averages afford
no distinct indice of crime, as to its causes, prevalence,
and character. What is needed, is not simply to know
what is the average criminality of a district, or county, but
its character,—its reference to age, condition, and habits
of life. By means only of an accurate and close analysis can these be known; and being known, the causes
of crime may be arrived at, and its preventives and cure
be devised.

In order to arrive at this analysis of crime, the following
process has been adopted, with reference to 37 counties of
England—Northumberland, Westmoreland, and Cumberland being disregarded, as so peculiar and distinct in their
organization, social and industrial, as only to perplex and
disturb any broad general conclusions.

In the first place, the proportions of the population in
each, at the several sections of age already noted, have
been ascertained, according to the census of 1841; and
also the proportions for the same sections of age *for all
England*. Next, assuming the ratio of increase in the
population from 1841 to 1845, to be same as from 1831
to 1841, the population of each county in 1845 has been
calculated; and then, taking the number of criminals at
each section of age, the criminality of each county has
been ascertained, after adjusting the population, in each
section of age, to the average of all England. The following Table shows the result of this combined process :—

TABLE VII.—Showing the Percentage of the Population at the undermentioned Ages, the Crime at each Age, the Total Average of Actual Crime, and the Average of Crime, after adjusting the ratios of Ages to the Average of all England. Average, 1844—6.

COUNTY.	Juveniles.		Adults. 20 years and under 25.		Adults. 25 years and under 30.		Adults. 30 years and upwards.		Total of all ages.	
	Proportion to all the Population.	Crime, One in	Proportion to all the Population.	Crime, One in	Proportion to all the Population.	Crime, One in	Proportion to all the Population.	Crime, One in	Crime, One in	Crime corrected for age one in
Bedford	48·	1184	9·5	211	7·4	399	35·1	687	645	637
Berkshire	45·7	961	9·2	221	7·6	336	37·5	819	634	627
Bucks	46·9	861	8·9	206	7·4	257	36·8	726	564	553
Cambridge	47·8	1275	9·9	232	7·6	292	34·7	700	642	640
Chester	47·6	920	10·1	263	8·1	300	34·2	581	569	569
Cornwall	49·	2381	8·9	516	7·1	580	35·	1354	1317	1275
Derby	47·4	2354	9·2	465	7·8	535	35·6	1143	1168	1150
Devon	45·5	1454	9·2	304	7·5	329	37·8	815	766	756
Dorset	47·	1450	8·8	340	7·2	451	37·	842	846	844
Durham	47·5	2805	10·	507	8·2	628	34·3	1274	1305	1310
Essex	47·	873	9·2	231	7·5	356	36·3	740	610	602
Gloucester	45·	566	9·7	208	7·9	315	37·4	608	469	470
Hereford	43·9	1175	8·7	179	7·4	250	40·	639	561	553
Hertford	47·	1111	9·3	240	7·5	407	36·2	656	647	642
Hunts	47·1	1146	9·6	243	7·5	414	35·8	992	742	731
Kent	45·3	1141	9·7	249	7·7	312	37·3	851	680	680
Lancaster	47·	973	10·4	281	8·7	352	33·9	664	621	628
Leicester	46·7	781	9·2	226	7·5	323	36·6	731	576	570
Lincoln	46·5	1730	9·5	282	7·	343	37·	1013	851	835
Middlesex	40·	433	11·	189	9·8	290	39·2	513	383	390
Monmouth	44·8	1156	10·9	241	9·	368	35·3	622	605	627
Norfolk	46·2	833	9·1	222	7·2	316	37·5	743	589	579
Northampton	46·5	1560	9·3	244	7·4	284	36·8	820	722	709
Notts	46·6	1215	9·	309	7·9	644	36·5	1034	869	861
Oxford	46·8	1068	9·3	233	7·3	326	36·6	589	598	589
Rutland	46·5	2059	8·4	265	7·	386	38·1	939	886	882
Salop	46·1	1363	9·1	315	7·6	397	37·2	719	749	744
Somerset	45·7	760	9·4	204	7·5	280	37·4	613	516	512
Southampton	45·5	915	9·7	245	7·8	333	37·	887	648	648
Stafford	48·5	1204	9·6	301	8·2	340	33·7	682	687	680
Suffolk	47·2	851	9·	218	7·2	292	36·6	1030	638	625
Surrey	42·	789	9·9	255	8·6	451	39·5	989	664	666
Sussex	47·5	1208	9·1	286	7·5	389	35·9	767	728	712
Warwick	45·7	656	9·9	206	8·4	357	36·	750	529	532
Worcester	46·4	636	9·2	156	7·6	230	36·8	535	428	433
Wilts	46·9	991	9·1	235	7·	327	37·	758	655	625
York, County	47·7	1891	9·6	440	7·9	524	34·8	1165	1088	1077
Ditto, E. Riding	44·3	2354	10·2	465	8·2	535	37·3	1143	1168	1160
Ditto, N. Riding	45·	2805	9·2	507	7·5	628	38·3	1274	1305	1302
Ditto, W. Riding	49·	1892	9·6	426	7·9	500	33·5	1128	1068	1045
All England	45·8	971	9·7	262	8·	363	36·5	753	641	

One great fact is patent on the face of this Table, namely, that with the same, or nearly the same *average* criminality, the criminality *at the several sections of age* is most discrepant and diverse. Three instances have already been noticed ; four more may usefully be pointed out.

COUNTY.	Under 20 yrs. of age, 1 in.	20 to 25 yrs. of age, 1 in	25 to 30 yrs. of age, 1 in	30 years and upwards, 1 in
Norfolk - - -	833	222	316	743
Oxford - - -	1068	233	326	589
Leicester - -	781	226	323	731
Chester - - -	920	263	300	581

The total average criminality is as under :—

> Norfolk - - - - - 1 in 589
> Oxford - - - - - 1 in 598
> Leicester- - - - - 1 in 576
> Chester - - - - - 1 in 569

It needs no deep philosophy to perceive that there must be some great difference in the social condition, at the several sections of ages, and in the temptations to which they are severally exposed ; and it is with the intention of drawing attention to these striking peculiarities, so that the causes of them may be, *if possible, ascertained,* that they are so minutely pointed out. It is mere empiricism to group counties, on account of similar general organization, or of equal absolute crime, to all the population. Averages are most deceptive. Science asks for *means,* all other things being alike ! It is quite clear, from the Table given, that averages cover most dissimilar circumstances and results, and therefore afford no safe data for concluding for or against particular organizations, social or industrial. *Analysis* points to influences *most dissimilar,* where the general average is alike, and thus indicates the rule of investigation—namely, to detect the special incidence of particular organizations, out of which such dissimilar results arise.

It would be idle or impertinent, in the present state of our knowledge, to attempt even to point out these particular incidences; suffice it now to give a Table of the facts.

Table 8 gives the order of criminality at each section of age, for the thirty-seven counties.   The counties embraced in the Table comprise six manufacturing counties, and the twenty-two agricultural, compared in the preceding chapter; and also the two metropolitan counties—Middlesex and Surrey; three mining counties—Cornwall, Durham, and Monmouth; and four mixed counties—Derby, Notts, Gloucester, and Worcester.   The position of the manufacturing counties, under each section of age, is indicated by CAPITALS, and in accordance with the design of this chapter, that position is now noticed.

The West Riding of York maintains a high position throughout; and it must be remembered that the calculation of criminality in it is based on a most fair distribution of the crime of the entire county, amongst the several Ridings.   The position of Stafford is also remarkable, and that of Lancaster scarcely less so.   Chester stands next, and then Leicester and Warwick.

TABLE VIII.—Showing the order of Criminality at each of the undermentioned Sections of Age in the undermentioned Counties. Average, 1844—6.

Juvenile Crime.	Ratio to Pop. One in	Crime, 20 to 25.	Ratio to Pop. One in	Crime, 25 to 30.	Ratio to Pop. One in	Crime, 30 and upwards.	Ratio to Pop. One in
Durham	2805	Cornwall	516	Notts ...ı.....	644	Cornwall	1354
York. N. R.	2805	Durham	507	Durham......	628	Durham......	1274
Cornwall	2381	York, N. R.	507	York, N. R.	628	York,N.R. ..	1274
Derby	2384	Derby	465	Cornwall	580	York,County	1165
York, E. R.	2354	York, E. R.	465	Derby	535	Derby	1143
Rutland	2059	York, County	440	York, E. Rid.	535	York, E.R...	1143
YORK, w.ʀ.	1892	YORK, w.ʀ.	426	York, County	524	YORK, w.ʀ.	1128
York, County	1891	Dorset..........	340	YORK, w.ʀ.	500	Notts	1034
Lincoln	1730	Salop	315	Dorset.........	451	Suffolk	1030
Northamptn.	1560	Notts	309	Surrey.........	451	Lincoln	1013
Devon........	1454	Devon........	304	Hunts.........	414	Hunts........	992
Dorset.........	1450	STAFFORD	301	Hertford......	407	Surrey.........	989
Salop	1363	Sussex	286	Bedford	399	Rutland	939
Cambridge...	1275	Lincoln	282	Salop.	397	Southamptn.	887
Notts	1215	LANCSTR.	281	Rutland	386	Keɴt..........	851
Sussex	1208	Rutland	265	Sussex	389	Dorset.........	842
STAFFORD	1204	CHESTER.	263	Monmouth...	368	Northamptn.	820
Bedford	1184	Surrey.........	255	WARWICK	357	Berkshire ...	819
Hereford ...	1175	Kent	249	Essex	356	Devon	815
Monmouth ..	1156	Northamptn.	244	LANCSTR.	352	Sussex........	767
Hunts........	1146	Hunts...ᴀ...	243	Lincoln	343	Wilts	758
Kent	1141	Southamptn.	245	STAFFORD	340	WARWICK	750
Hertford......	1111	Monmouth. .	241	Berkshire ...	336	Norfolk	743
Oxford	1068	Hertford......	240	Southamptn.	333	Essex	740
Wilts	991	Wilts	235	Devon........	329	LEICESTR.	731
LANCSTR..	973	Oxford	233	Wilts	327	Bucks	726
Berkshire ...	961	Cambridge ...	232	Oxford	326	Salop	719
CHESTER..	920	Essex	231	LEICESTR.	323	Cambridge...	700
Southamptn.	915	LEICESTR.	226	Norfolk	316	Bedford	687
Essex	873	Norfolk	222	Gloucester ...	315	STAFFORD	682
Bucks	861	Berkshire ...	221	Kent	312	LANCSTR.	664
Suffolk	851	Suffolk	218	CHESTER..	300	Hereford	639
Norfolk	833	Bedford	211	Cambridge...	292	Hertford......	656
Surrey.........	789	Gloucester...	208	Suffolk	292	Monmouth..	622
LEICESTR.	781	Bucks.........	206	Middlesex ...	290	Somerset ...	613
Somerset ...	761	Somerset ...	204	Northamptn.	284	Gloucester...	608
WARWICK	656	WARWICK	206	Somerset	280	Oxford	589
Worcester ...	636	Middlesex ...	189	Bucks.........	257	CHESTER.	581
Gloucester ...	566	Hereford	179	Hereford	250	Worcester...	535
Middlesex ...	433	Worcester....	156	Worcester....	230	Middlesex ...	513
All England	971	All England	262	All England	363	All England	753

One great fact is made out by this Table—namely, that no broad conclusion in favour of the morality of either set of counties, agricultural or manufacturing, is fairly deducible from it. It is quite evident that no one agricultural county can be named, as high in morality (morality being indicated by crime), but a manufacturing county may be also named, paralleling it in all respects. In fact, the most purely agricultural counties stand in juxtaposition with the most purely manufacturing, at each section of age, and are at disadvantage in the comparison. In juvenile criminality, Lincoln is lower than the West Riding, and Berkshire than Lancashire. In adult crime, at its earlier stages, Dorset is lower than the West Riding, Lincoln than Stafford; Kent than Lancaster, and Norfolk than Leicester. In the next section of age, the West Riding of York maintains the same position to Dorset; Warwick, Lancaster, and Stafford, are below Berkshire, Devon, and Oxford; and Leicester and Chester are before Cambridge and Suffolk. In the last section, the West Riding still heads Lincoln; Warwick, Norfolk, Leicester, Bucks, Stafford, and Lancaster, are before Hereford, Hertford, and Somerset; and Chester alone stands low in the scale of the manufacturing counties.

Nothing could more distinctly show the impertinence and folly of such groupings of counties, as Mr. Fletcher and Mr. Symons have followed, than this Table. The former places York, Notts, Derby, Worcester, and Gloucester in his group of manufacturing counties! No one can look at the position of these respectively, under these four sections of ages, but must see that the grouping is most absurd and unphilosophical; and Mr. Symons is scarcely less in error in classing together Lancashire and

Cheshire, as forming the Cotton district; and Derby, Leicester, and Notts, as forming the Silk, Wool, and Hosiery districts respectively. The force of folly, prejudice, and absurdity could scarcely go further. In fact, by grouping counties, any absurdity may be maintained. A sound philosophy demands a more rigid and separate investigation, such as these gentlemen have thought proper to eschew.

Touching the second part, the proportion of the classes, it has already been observed, more than once, that the great mass of the offences cognizable at the assizes and the quarter sessions, is committed by the operative classes; and by a class, which is, *per se*, the criminal class. It is obvious, that the amount of criminal offences will be in the highest ratio, other things being alike, in those counties in which the operative classes are aggregated in the highest proportion; and as it is in the large towns and cities principally, that the criminal class find their prey, and their places of concealment also, it follows, that wherever the operative class exists, in a proportion to the whole population above the average, and the town and city population is in the same category, there, *cæteris paribus*, crime will be most abundant.

The "OCCUPATIONS ABSTRACT," and the "Age Abstract" of the census of 1841, furnish the means of determining the relative numbers of the classes in question, except as respects the criminal class; the numbers of which only admit, as will be shown, of conjecture. The former document shows the following proportions, for four principal classes, constituting in fact the actually working population of the country :—

Persons engaged in trade and manufacture -	16·9
Labourers - - - - - -	4·2
Persons engaged in agriculture - - -	7·7
Domestic servants - - - - -	6·2
	35·0
Town population - - - - -	59·0
Rural ditto - - - - -	41·0
	100·0

It is believed, that the four classes enumerated furnish the vast majority of the criminal offenders. The figures are taken from the 22nd page of the " Occupations Abstract."

It may perhaps be objected, that the 1st and 3rd heads comprise persons of the middle class, as well as labourers, artisans, and servants. The fact is not denied; but in a comparison betwixt the manufacturing and the agricultural counties, the inclusion of the middle class is of no moment in determining the question of comparative morality, because the inclusion is common to both classes of the population,—the 1st column comprising all the retail and wholesale dealers, master manufacturers, clerks, &c.; and the 3rd column comprising farmers and graziers. True, if the proportions of the middle class to the whole of each section respectively, are not alike, that will cause an error in the solution of the question at issue; but the difference of proportion cannot be so great, as materially to affect the integrity and value of that solution.

The proportions of each of these classes have been

taken from the " Occupations Abstract," and the result shows, that in the six principal manufacturing counties, there is an excess of from 0·9 to 5·1 centesimal parts above the average of all England ; and that the 22 principal agricultural counties are all below the average of England, in various degrees, varying from 0·5 to 5·8 centesimal parts. Four other counties, which are partly manufacturing and partly agricultural, exhibit a range of deviation from the average of England, extending from 2·3 above, to 4·4 below it.

Taking into account the relative populations, and the relative excess or deficiency of the operative classes, as compared with the average of England in the three groups of counties, the manufacturing group may be considered as averaging 2 per cent. above the average of all England, and the agricultural group 2 per cent. under it. If, then, the influence of age, as affecting the amount of crime, be first eliminated, and 2 per cent. be added to the ratio of criminality shown in the agricultural, and 2 per cent. deducted from the criminality of the manufacturing, the true comparative ratio of criminality will be ascertained;—saving that, the action of a criminal class fostered and harboured in the immense town and city populations of the latter, will yet have to be estimated. That will, for the present, be disregarded, but will be treated of in the course of the chapter.

The first step in the process, then, is to adjust crime according to the relative proportions of the population at the several ages, in each group of counties. In order to this, the proportions of the ages, as shown by the census of 1841, have been ascertained for all England, and for seven groups of counties, as under:—

F

GROUPS OF COUNTIES.	Proportions of the under-mentioned ages to the total population, in each group of counties, and in all England.				
	Under 20.	20 and under 25.	25 and under 30.	30 and above.	TOTAL.
* Six Manufacturing Counties	47·8	9·9	8·3	34·	100
† Twenty-two Agricultural do.	46·3	9·3	7·3	37·1	100
‡ Three Mining do.	45·4	9·6	7·8	37·2	100
§ Five other do.	46·4	9·3	7·8	36·5	100
Gloucester and Worcester -	45·4	9·5	7·8	37·3	100
Middlesex- - - - - -	40·	11·	9·8	39·2	100
Surrey- - - - - - -	42·	9·9	8·6	39·5	100
All England - - - -	45·8	9·7	8·	36·5	100

The next step is to divide the population in each group according to the proportions shown above, assuming, of course, that the proportions had not altered in 1844, 1845, and 1846. And having further ascertained the number of offences corresponding to each section of ages, to determine the ratio of criminality in each section. The following Table exhibits the result :—

GROUPS OF COUNTIES.	Ratio of Criminality at the ages undermentioned in 1845 (average of 1844 and 1846.)				
	Under 20. 1 in	20 and under 25. 1 in	25 and under 30. 1 in	30 and above. 1 in	Average of all ages. 1 in
Six Manufacturing Counties	1114	302	386	780	710
Twenty-two Agricultural do.	1096	243	321	764	659
Three Mining do.	2184	420	540	1103	1103
Five other do.	1874	436	422	1419	1110
Gloucester and Worcester -	600	186	550	461	454
Middlesex - - - - -	433	189	290	513	383
Surrey - - - - - -	789	255	451	989	664
All England - - - -	971	262	363	753	641

* Cheshire, Lancaster, Leicester, Stafford, Warwick, and York.
† Bedford, Berks, Bucks, Cambridge, Devon, Dorset, Essex, Hereford, Hertford, Hunts, Kent, Lincoln, Northampton, Norfolk, Oxford, Rutland, Salop, Somerset, Southampton, Suffolk, Sussex, and Wilts.
‡ Cornwall, Durham, and Monmouth.
§ Cumberland, Derby, Northampton, Notts, Wilts, and Westmoreland.

This Table and the preceding furnish data on which the exact relative criminality of each group may be ascertained. For the purposes of this chapter, it is, however, only needful to calculate the criminality of the two first groups, by first reducing the total population to the same proportions of the several ages, as is shown for all England; and then, second, to calculate the number of offences at each age, according to the ratio of criminality in each, as shown above. The result may be thus stated : —

Corrected Ratio of Criminality in the under-mentioned Group of Counties.

    Six manufacturing counties -   -   -   1 in 710
    Twenty agricultural counties   -   -   1 in 649

Expressed, as before, in the number of criminals to each 100,000 of the population, the two groups will stand thus:—

        Manufacturing counties   -   -   -   140
        Agricultural counties -   -   -   -   154

Deducting 2 per cent. from the former group, and adding 2 per cent. to the latter, to bring them to the average of England, as respects the proportions of the operative classes, the numbers will stand, 137 and 157 : in other words, each 100,000 persons in the manufacturing counties furnishes 137 criminals, and the same number in the agricultural counties furnishes 157 criminals. The criminality of the latter is then greater by about 14 per cent. than the former.

It is believed that the process by which this result has been obtained, is strictly philosophical, and that the substantial accuracy of the results cannot be questioned. If

F 2

so, the fact is now patent, which men, not blinded by
prejudice, and not having their mental vision intercepted
by foregone conclusions, have for sometime strongly
surmised; viz., that the morality of the manufacturing
population ranks above the agricultural; and it must be
borne in especial remembrance, that in this comparison
no allowance is made for the incidence on crime of the
incessant immigration of the worst classes of the Irish
population into the manufacturing districts, nor for the
amount of crime committed in those districts by the predatory classes, who find plunder and refuge there, but
have no affinity with the indigenous and operative classes.
If the incidence of these two disturbing causes could be
estimated, little doubt exists that the ratio of crime in the
manufacturing districts would exhibit a far more favourable character.

The comparison instituted, comprises twenty-eight of
the forty counties of England. The Table on page 97
includes nine more, four of which, Derby, Notts, Gloucester, and Worcester, are included by Mr. Fletcher in
his 8th group of manufacturing and mining counties. It
may be necessary to state why they are not so classed in
these pages. The rule adopted in classing the counties
as manufacturing and agricultural respectively, has been
to rank those as manufacturing, in which the proportion
of the population engaged in trade and manufactures, and
as *labourers*, considerably exceeded the average of all
England; and to rank as agricultural, those in which the
proportion of persons engaged in agriculture exceeded the
average of England. The proportions of these several
classes of the population in the counties thrown out
of the two principal groups, are as follows :—

COUNTY.	Engaged in Commerce, Trade, and Manufactures	Labourers.	Total.	Engaged in Agriculture.
Derby - - - -	18·9	5·7	24·4	7·7
Notts - - - -	20·6	2·2	22·8	8·2
Gloucester- - -	15·1	5·	20·1	7·2
Worcester - -	16·7	3·9	20·6	10·1
All England - -	16·9	4·2	21·1	7·7

It is quite clear, as respects the three last-named counties, that they cannot be ranked either with the manufacturing or agricultural section. Derby might fairly be ranked with the former section, if the proportion of its *town population* corresponded with the total of the classes engaged in trade, &c., and as *labourers*. In fact, the total of these two classes in Derbyshire, is within four of the total of the same classes in Warwick; but the town population of Warwickshire is 14 per cent. above the average of England, whilst that of Derby is 18½ below. The composition of the population of Derbyshire is peculiar, and, to rank it with either the one or the other class previously compared, would only be to introduce an element of error. The peculiarity of its composition seems to explain the low ratio of crime; and the same remark applies to Notts. The high range of crime in Gloucester and Worcester is not satisfactorily solved by reference to the nature and proportions of the population of each; though it is not improbable that the crime of Bristol, which is very considerable, gives an unenviably high ratio to Gloucestershire, which would not exist if the same classes of each county could be compared together. As to Worcester, it is evident that some special deteriorating influence has been at work since 1801. In that year it stood 18, amongst the forty counties of England, in the order of crime, 1 being the *lowest ratio;* in 1821 it had fallen to 32; in 1831 it had risen to 25; in 1841 it again fell to 38; and in 1845 and 1848 it has remained lowest in the scale—excepting only Middlesex.

The remaining seven counties must now be noticed. The details, same as in the preceding Tables, are as follows :—

COUNTY.	Percentage of Persons employed in Trade and Manufactures.	Percentage of Labourers.	Percentage of Persons engaged in Agriculture.	Percentage of Domestic Servants.	Total of Preceding Classes.	Above the average of England.	Below the average of England.	Town Population.	Country Population.	Ratio of Crime, 1 in
Cumberland.	14·6	3·9	8·8	6·6	33·9	...	1·1	78·134	99·904	1323
Cornwall	9·3	8·9	7·9	5·9	32·	...	3·	12¹·469	218·810	1236
Durham	13·9	8·5	4·4	4·7	31·5	...	3·5	200·603	123·681	1276
Northum-⎫ berland. ⎭	14·9	6·2	6·9	5·6	33·6	...	1·4	164·843	85·435	1208
Westmore-⎫ land...... ⎭	13·8	2·3	11·6	7·6	35·3	·8	...	19·746	36·708	1160
Surrey	16·2	5·5	4·4	7·6	33·7	...	1·3	453·942	128·736	851
Monmouth ..	13·1	12·5	6·5	5·6	37·7	2·7	...	89·596	44·759	650
*All England	16·9	4·2	6·2	7·7	35·	...	...	...	...	...

The reasons for excluding these counties from any comparison of the manufacturing with the agricultural counties, are, it is believed, perfectly valid. Surrey may be disposed of with the remark, that more than one-half of its population is congregated around London, and, in fact, forms part of the metropolis. The county belongs to a different category; and it would only confuse and complicate the question under consideration, to place it with either of those classes. The sources and character of crime are quite distinct, and demand a separate and distinct kind of analysis. Monmouth is, in one sense, a manufacturing county; but there is a great peculiarity in the composition of its population—namely, the very large proportion of labourers, a class which furnishes a greater absolute and relative proportion of criminals, than any one of the three other classes enumerated. Durham, Cornwall, and Northumberland are mining counties, peculiar in their social and industrial organization, and cannot be classed either as manufacturing or agricultural. The lower ratio of crime in these counties is a phenomenon worthy of a close analysis, the materials for which, however, are not very apparent. Cumberland and Westmoreland are essentially agricultural counties; but there is this peculiarity in the composition of the population, that the class of farmers and graziers constitutes a very large proportion. It needs no argument to prove the position, that the class of small proprietors is one peculiarly exempt from the temptation to commit the kind of offences which come before the judicial tribunals of the country. Inducements to industry, sobriety, order, and to correct moral conduct in general, are strong in this class of the community; and, as respects the principal class of offences, larceny, and other forms of dishonesty, there is scarcely a temptation : and to meet such possible temptation as may be presented, the most powerful dissuasives from compliance,—the total loss of social status,—the certain destruction of reputation, and abiding shame, dishonour, and ruin of family. The following Table shows the percentage which the two great classes of persons engaged in agriculture bear to the total of persons so occupied in the two counties, and also in the manufacturing counties :—

Engaged in Agriculture.

COUNTY.	Farmers and Graziers. Number Per Cent.	Labourers. Number Per Cent.	Gardeners, &c. Number Per Cent.	Total.
Cumberland - -	33·6	64·6	1·8	100
Westmoreland -	37·8	60·5	1·7	100

Manufacturing Counties.

Cheshire - -	27·8	68·9	3·3	100
Lancashire - -	33·6	61·7	4·7	100
Leicester - - -	21·5	74·7	3·8	100
Stafford - - -	22·4	74·1	3·5	100
Warwick - - -	15·7	79·5	4·8	100
West Riding of York - - -	34·0	61·5	4·5	100
All England - -	18·3	77·8	3·9	100

It does not admit of a doubt that the high percentage of the first class of persons engaged in agriculture, namely, farmers and graziers, relatively to the second class, the labourers, must greatly affect the amount of crime; and it is worthy of especial notice that similar proportions of those classes in the West Riding of York, and in Lancashire, are also accompanied by a low absolute percentage of crime in the first county, and by a percentage of crime in the latter county, which must be considered very low relatively to the immense town population, the deteriorating influence of Irish immigration, and the excess of crime, in its great *seaport*, Liverpool. It is worthy of observation, too, that Derby, which presents a similar organization of its agricultural population,—the proportions being 36·2 and 60·9 respectively, is remarkable for the low average of its criminality.

It has been conclusively proved, that the six chief manufacturing counties are considerably less criminal, regard being had to the *total of crime*, than the agricultural. If the comparison, however, terminated here, it would be most incomplete, and some valuable and important corroborations of the theory which assigns a large proportion of the crime against property to the aggregation of vast masses of the population in large towns and cities, in juxtaposition with great wealth and luxury, would be overlooked. For the purpose, then, of a more minute comparison, and with a view to determine, if practicable, whether particular social and industrial forms of organization exhibit peculiar phases and proportions of crime, the crime of each section of the counties has been analyzed under the same head, as in the First Chapter, omitting only the 2nd Class, " Assaults," and the 7th Class, " Riots and Sedition," both because they form only a small portion of the total of crime, and because they do not exhibit any marked difference of ratios, comparing the two sections ; though the excess, in each class of crime, is on the side of the agricultural counties. In the following Table, the figures under the several columns or classes of crime, are millionth parts ; that is, supposing the population in each county to be one million, the ratio of the actual offences of each class, to the actual population, would give so many offences of that class.

So high a numeral has been taken, in order to avoid minute proportions, which do not present so distinct an idea of relative quantities as larger numbers.

Table IX.—Showing the Ratio, in Millionth Parts, of the under-mentioned Classes of Offences, in the Counties named, and the Total Ratio of Offences against Property, without Violence; the latter being the Summary of Classes 4, 5, 6, and 8.

CLASS I. Serious Offences.		CLASS III. Offences against Property, with Violence.		CLASS IV. Simple Larcenies.		CLASS V. All other Larcenies.		CLASS VI. Embezlements, Fraud, &c.		CLASS VIII. All other Offences.		SUMMARY. Classes iv. v. vi. and viii.	
Derby	41	Dorset	54	Derby	429	Lincoln	55	Rutland	13	Rutland	3	Derby	623
YORK, w.r.	41	Devon	58	Notts	450	Southmptn	62	Notts	26	WARWICK	31	Notts	664
Lincoln	52	Salop	61	York, Co.	468	Cambridge	72	Derby	38	YORK, w.r.	45	York, Co.	678
York, Co.	53	Hunts	65	YORK, w.r.	600	Hunts	82	York, Co.	46	STAFFORD	49	Rutland	783
Notts	56	STAFFORD	65	Hunts	677	Dorset	87	Northmptn.	55	York, Co.	53	YORK, w.r.	835
Salop	56	Notts	76	Rutland	736	Rutland	90	Devon	69	Derby	56	Lincoln	958
WARWICK	57	YORK, w.r.	76	Dorset	747	Suffolk	91	Salop	72	Southamptn.	58	Dorset	991
LANCAST.	66	Lincoln	80	Kent	816	Salop	92	Hertford	72	Devon	59	Hunts	1065
Devon	69	Northmptn.	81	Hunts	821	Derby	100	Lincoln	75	LANCAST.	62	Devon	1108
Berks	71	Wilts	82	Bedford	835	Devon	100	Kent	75	CHESTER	63	Northmptn.	1140
Sussex	71	Derby	86	LANCAST.	842	Northmptn.	105	Dorset	76	Hunts	64	Salop	1176
Southamptn.	73	Sussex	86	Sussex	871	York, Co.	111	Southmptn	77	Notts	69	Cambridge	1181
Kent	75	York, Co.	88	Northamptn.	872	Norfolk	118	Cambridge	78	Oxford	72	STAFFORD	1192

Hereford.....	78	Berks	89	Devon.........	880	Notts	119	Hereford....	78	Berks	78	Kent	1221
Oxford	78	Kent	91	Essex	888	Oxford	132	Bedford	79	Kent	78	Bedford	1223
LEICEST. .	80	Oxford	96	Hertford......	894	Berks	142	STAFFORD	83	Suffolk	78	Suffolk	1229
Dorset........	82	Southamptn	98	Cambridge...	899	Bucks	143	Essex	89	Salop	80	Berks	1260
Hunts.........	82	Norfolk	99	STAFFORD	916	STAFFORD	144	Wilts	90	Dorget	81	Hertford	1285
Somerset ...	86	CHESTER.	101	Salop	932	Wilts	150	YORK,w.r.	90	Essex	83	Essex	1303
Wilts	86	Hertford......	104	Berks	945	Somerset.....	158	Worcester ...	94	Sussex	84	Wilts	1304
STAFFORD	89	Gloucester...	104	Suffolk	966	Hereford.....	164	Suffolk	94	Wilts	85	Southmptn..	1305
Rutland......	90	LANCAST..	107	Wilts	979	LEICESTR.	178	Berks	95	LEICESTR.	86	LANCAST.	1307
Northamptn.	91	Bedford	114	Bucks.........	1014	Hertford......	196	Hunts	98	Sussex	92	Sussex	13?1
Hertford.....	92	Cambridge...	115	LEICESTR.	1026	YORK,w.r.	200	LEICESTR.	102	Bucks	97	Bucks	1391
CHESTER.	94	Suffolk	124	Hereford	1042	Bedford	211	Bucks.........	106	Norfolk	104	LEICESTR.	1392
Gloucester..	95	Rutland	135	CHESTER.	1058	CHESTER.	212	Oxford	108	Northmptn...	108	Oxford	1404
Bucks.........	100	Essex	145	Norfolk	1074	Essex	248	CHESTER.	115	Worcester ...	122	Norfolk	1414
Worcester ...	115	LEICESTR.	151	WARWICK	1078	Kent	252	WARWICK	116	Hertford	123	Hereford	1437
Essex.........	117	WARWICK	152	Oxford	1092	WARWICK	266	Norfolk	118	Bucks	128	CHESTER.	1447
Bedford	123	Somerset ...	162	Somerset ...	1092	Sussex	274	LANCAST..	127	Cambridge..	132	WARWICK	1491
Cambridge ..	132	Bucks.........	163	Southamptn.	1108	LANCAST..	276	Somerset ...	128	Somerset....	139	Somerset ...	1517
Norfolk	135	Hereford.....	199	Gloucester ..	1290	Worcester ...	316	Sussex	132	Hereford	153	Worcester ...	1846
Suffolk	158	Worcester ...	247	Worcester ..	1314	Gloucester ..	353	Gloucester...	148	Gloucester...	159	Gloucester...	1950
Middlesex...	82	....	90	....	1222	....	593	....	165	....	106	....	2086
All England.	77	....	95	....	873	....	212	....	94	....	88	....	1267

Before offering any remarks on the indications of this
Table, it is needful to explain that the ratios under each section
of offences, and for each county or group of counties, have
undergone no correction for the excess or deficiency, either
of persons betwixt fifteen and thirty years of age, or of the
purely operative population.

The correction of the total number of offences in each
county, for such excess or deficiency, would be perfectly
legitimate. But if it be desired to correct the ratios of particular offences, correspondingly with the correction of the
total numbers, the inquiry presents itself, — Does the
excess or deficiency, in one or both particulars, affect all
classes of crime equally ; or does it affect them unequally,
—and if unequally, what is the measure of the inequality ?
Nay, more, the question must be asked,—Does it affect all
kinds of offences, or only some ; and if some, which ? Analogy suggests that such offences as spring from hot blood,
strong passion, and immature judgment, would be most
rife, where the population from fifteen to thirty was the
greatest ; but analogy cannot be trusted in a matter of
rigorous analytical induction. The Table, therefore, must
be understood as exhibiting the actual proportions of each
class of offences ; but the ratios shown for each county, or
group of counties, considered relatively to the ratios of other
counties or groups of counties, must be held subject to correction for the incidence of age and population. It has been
shown already, that the result of such correction, as applied
to six manufacturing and twenty-two agricultural counties,
produces the figures 137 and 157 respectively, as the number
of persons in each 100,000 of the population annually
sent to the assizes or quarter sessions; or, in other
words, the agricultural counties furnish seven criminals to

every six furnished by the manufacturing counties. The position of the manufacturing counties under each class of offences, is indicated by CAPITALS, not only for a more ready comparison with the agricultural, but in order that it may steadily be kept in view, that the actual position is not the true one,—the true one on the average of all the classes of crime, being one-seventh higher in the scale.

Six classes of crime are analyzed in the Table. If their efficient causes, however, be regarded, the six resolve into two classes—Nos. 1 and 3 constituting a class of crimes, which spring from unbridled passions, malice, or ferocity of disposition ; and Nos. 4 to 6 and 8, constituting a second class, originating in a lawless or avaricious disregard of the right to property.

Respect for life and property is so essential to the well-being, and almost the existence of a community, that the degree in which the criminal calendar of any country measures that respect, is regarded as a principal and important criterion, by which to estimate its civilization and morality. It may admit, however, of grave doubt, whether the criterion by itself is of much value. To judge of a nation's morality by its criminal calendar alone, is to judge of it by the small fraction of what is bad, and to throw out of the scale the great mass of what is good. It is only another form of the old fallacy of judging a whole by a small part. The statistics of crime do not so much help to measure the morality of a nation, as they help to measure the degree of the morality of particular classes,—the depth in the social strata to which religious influences have penetrated, and the counteracting force of the evil influences springing out of great luxury and wealth, in juxtaposition with a great preponderance of the very lowest classes ; those classes being comparatively isolated from the more refined, educated, and moral sections of the community. In commenting upon the several classes of crime enumerated in the Table, the spirit of these observations must be borne in mind. The ratios of criminal offenders to the whole population of particular counties, must not be taken as positive indices of the moral status of its entire population, but as indices of influences and causes, acting upon particular classes. To overlook this great rule in such investigations, is just to omit the most nice and delicate process in the analysis,—the detection of the incidences of particular occupations, density of population, and the proportions of sexes and ages, in increasing or decreasing criminal offences, whilst the moral tone and character of the classes who constitute, so to speak, the staple of a county, are comparatively unaffected.

The first column of the Table places the manufacturing counties high in the scale, three counties ranging below the average of England, and three above it,—the greatest excess being about 22 per cent. The agricultural counties, on the other hand, place seven counties under, and fifteen above the average of England, the greatest excess being upwards of 100 per cent. If the opinion be correct,—and it is not without great appearance of truth,—that the more serious offences are generally committed by the indigenous, or, at all events, the permanently resident population of the localities in which they occur, the very high ratios of these offences in so large a proportion of the agricultural counties, appears indicative of great brutality of manners, and great moral degradation amongst a considerable portion of the lowest class. It is true that, relatively to the whole population, the ratio of such offences is small; but it must always be borne in mind that the grosser forms of offences are alone cognisable by the tribunals, and these may be considered as types only of a considerable number of offences, of the same generic character, which, however, do not come within the pale of legal questioning and punishment.

The 3rd class of crime may be briefly dismissed. Burglaries, house-breaking, and robberies from the person, accompanied with threats or violence, stand opposed to the serious offences, in one important respect,—that they are, in the main, committed by a migratory class of criminals; and the prevalence, or otherwise, of this form of criminality in particular counties, cannot be held as of much moment in determining their moral condition. It is notorious that London sends out its professional burglars and house-breakers into all parts of the provinces. It is a necessary part of the tactics of the class, to pounce upon localities unexpectedly; and it is obvious, from the nature of their depredations, and the hot pursuit which follows such offences, that a long stay in one neighbourhood, or county even, is not a little perilous.

Class 4. Simple larcenies, again, exhibit the agricultural counties in an unfavourable light. It is not a little extraordinary, to find the thinly-peopled agricultural counties exhibiting as high a degree of this form of dishonesty as the densely-populated manufacturing counties, where the opportunities and temptations to the offence are so much more numerous; but so it is. Here is the proof:—

Inhabit- ants to 100 Acres	County.	Ratio of Simple Larcenies.	Inhabit- ants to 100 Acres	County.	Ratio of Simple Larcenies.
70	York, W. Riding	1 in 600	21·7	Lincoln - -	1 in 736
147·5	Lancaster - -	1 in 842	31·9	Sussex - -	1 in 871
			32·2	Devon - -	1 in 880
67·4	Stafford - -	1 in 916	27·8	Salop - -	1 in 932
			33·5	Berks - -	1 in 945
41·9	Leicester - -	1 in 1026	33·	Bucks - -	1 in 1014
58·8	Chester - -	1 in 1058	31·9	Norfolk - -	1 in 1074
70·	Warwick -	1 in 1078	41·4	Somerset -	1 in 1092

The 5th Class. All other offences includes larcenies from dwelling-houses, above £5 in value, larcenies from the person, and larcenies by servants. The first of these is small in number, the other two are considerable. The analysis of the three years gives the following result.

Larcenies from the Person.

	Average Number of Offences.	Ratio to Pop.
6 Manufacturing counties - -	556 - -	1 in 8,470
22 Agricultural ditto - -	346 - -	1 in 16,753
Middlesex - - - - - -	562 - -	1 in 2,984
All England - - - - -	1752 - -	1 in 9,047

Larcenies by Servants.

6 Manufacturing counties - -	410 - -	1 in 11,486
22 Agricultural ditto - -	385 - -	1 in 15,056
Middlesex - - - -	355 -	1 in 4,725
All England - - -	1467 - -	1 in 10,817

It will excite no surprise that robberies from the person, in the manufacturing, are in a nearly double proportion to those of the agricultural counties. The cause is an obvious one, and little reliance can be placed on the respective ratios, as tests of the relative honesty of the really working classes. They only indicate, in the main, the proportions of the professional or habitual thieves found in each ;—a class which is an aggregation of the worst of all counties, and cannot properly be said to belong to any.

The honesty of servants appears to be higher in the agricultural than manufacturing counties, in the proportion of 15 to $11\frac{1}{2}$; but it is in reality much higher than these figures indicate, servants forming a proportion of the agricultural population, greater than in the manufacturing counties, in the ratio of 6·4 to 5·2. In round numbers, allowance being made for this difference, the relative proportions of larcenies by servants, would be as 18 to $11\frac{1}{2}$; or in other words, the honesty of servants is less in the latter than the former counties, by about 33 per cent. But the conclusion would not be warrantable, on these data, that respect for property amongst the classes of society, in the two groups of counties respectively, which furnish domestic and other servants, is in the same ratio as the honesty of servants ;—because it is a fact admitting of no dispute, that the majority of domestic servants (of which there are upwards of 200,000 males, and 712,000 females in England) are taken from the rural population. In fact, the young women born in the manufacturing towns, rarely enter into domestic service, preferring the comparative independence of factory labour.

The 6th class embraces embezzlements, receiving stolen goods, and frauds. For very obvious reasons, there is shown in the Table a preponderance of these offences in the manufacturing districts. Where offices of great trust are relatively most numerous, the occurrences of embez-

zlement will correspond; and as respects the other two
classes of offences, it needs no argument to prove, that,
from the vast accumulation and concentration of property
in the great seats of manufacture, the incentives to these
kinds of fraud are far more numerous, and the opportunity of concealing them, are far greater there, than in
the rural districts. Bearing in mind this fact, it does
appear strange, that whilst Stafford and the West Riding
of York are below the average of all England, Leicester
should exhibit a ratio so little above Suffolk, Berks, and
Huntingdon; and that Lancashire is less than either Somerset or Sussex.

The 8th Class comprises three sub-sections: 1st,
cattle, sheep, and horse-stealing,—2nd, forgery, and offences against the currency,—and, 3rd, being out armed at
night in pursuit of game, perjury, keeping disorderly
houses, and misdemeanors. For all England, in 1845,
the proportion of these sections of crime to the population, was 1 in 44·451, 36·231, and 40·074 respectively.
The following are the proportions for the manufacturing
and the agricultural counties respectively:—

	Sect. 1.	Sect. 2.	Sect. 3.
6 Manufacturing counties average - -	1 in 88·855	54·074	35·145
22 Agricultural counties ditto - - -	1 in 29·670	50·057	48·306

A threefold greater proportion of offences under the 1st
section, and a smaller proportion of the offences under the
3rd section, in the agricultural than in the manufacturing counties, is not surprising, considering the opportunities and temptations to each class of crimes, in the
respective divisions of counties; but a higher proportion

of forgeries, &c. in the agricultural counties is somewhat anomalous.

The concluding column exhibits the proportion to population of the aggregate offences, comprised under the four preceding ones. It is, in fact, the measure of criminality, with reference to PROPERTY, in each county, excluding such offences as are accompanied by violence to the person. It will suffice, with respect to this summary, to direct observation to the fact, that in juxtaposition with each of the manufacturing counties, there is found one or more of the agricultural, showing an equal or greater ratio of criminality. There is no broad line of demarcation in the respective degrees of criminality,—indeed, as will be seen in the next Table,—the ratios are all but identical, always observing, that there is no correction for the incidences of age and population.

For the sake of comparison, the following Table is given, exhibiting the ratios of the same classes of offences, as in Table, pages 106 and 107. Comment upon it is unnecessary, as, whatever indication of moment it contains, will fall under review in reference to the next Table.

Table X.—Showing the Ratio, in Millionth Parts, of the under-mentioned Classes of Offences, in the Counties named, and the Total Ratio of Offences against Property, without Violence; the latter being the Summary of Classes 4, 5, 6, and 8.

CLASS I. Serious Offences.	CLASS III. Offences against Property, with Violence.	CLASS IV. Simple Larcenies.	CLASS V. All other Larcenies.	CLASS VI. Embezzlements, Fraud, &c.	CLASS VIII. All other Offences.	SUMMARY. Classes IV. V. VI. and VIII.
Cornwall 50	Cornwall...... 19	Durham 393	Westmoreland 19	Westmoreland 34	Westmoreland 5	Durham 511
Westmoreland 52	Westmoreland 35	Northumberld. 407	Cornwall 27	Cornwall...... 42	Durham 30	Cumberland ... 570
Northumberld. 60	Cumberland ... 44	Cumberland ... 424	Durham 35	Northumberld. 47	Cumberland ... 32	Cornwall 599
Cumberland ... 60	Durham 47	Cornwall....... 489	Cumberland .. 38	Durham 52	Cornwall....... 41	Northumberld. 628
Surrey........ 75	Northumberld. 60	Westmoreland 664	Northumberld. 110	Monmouth 63	Northumberld. 64	Westmoreland. 717
Durham........ 86	Surrey 77	Surrey 764	Monmouth ... 149	Cumberland ... 76	Monmouth..... 84	Surrey 1242
Monmouth...... 93	Monmouth 100	Monmouth...... 1026	Surrey 253	Surrey.......... 83	Surrey........... 142	Monmouth..... 1322
All England. 77	 95	 873	 212	 94	 88	 1267

The analysis of the several classes of crime in the forty counties of England now presented, shows the respective proportions in millionth parts. That measure of relation was adopted as the best for the purpose in hand. But it does not convey an equally definite idea of the proportions of each class or kind of crime, to all other crimes, or to the population, as the more.common method of indicating the number of the population amongst whom *one* criminal of each class is annually brought before the tribunals. For the double purpose, then, of placing the ratio of criminality, absolute and relative, under each class of offences, in a more definite, and, so to speak, pictorial manner, before the mind, the following Table has been constructed ; in which, as the individual counties in the ·two groups—agricultural and manufacturing—have already been fully examined, and their mutual relations pointed out and explained, the averages only of each group are given.

Table XI.—Showing the Ratio of Offences to Population, under Six Heads or Classes, and the Total Offences under the Four Last, in the under-mentioned Counties and Groups of Counties, and for all England.

CLASS I. Serious Offences. 1 in		CLASS III. Offences against Property, with Violence. 1 in		CLASS IV. Simple Larcenies. 1 in		CLASS V. All other Larcenies. 1 in		CLASS VI. Embezlements, Fraud, &c. 1 in		CLASS VIII. All other Offences. 1 in		Summary of 4 last Classes. 1 in	
Derby	21·045	Cornwall	51·386	Durham	2537	Westmreld.	57·018	Notts	37·271	Durham	32·752	Durham	1947
Cornwall	19·883	Westmreld.	28·509	Northumb.	2453	Cornwall	35·970	Westmreld.	28·509	Cumberland	30·266	Cumberland	1746
Westmreld.	19·006	Cumberland	22·699	Cumberland	2384	Cumberland	25·799	Derby	26·231	Cornwall	23·980	Cornwall	1662
York, Co.	18·608	Durham	21·175	Derby	2327	Durham	27·713	Cornwall	23·980	Westmreld.	19·006	Derby	1585
Notts	17·392	Northumb.	16·408	Cornwall	2043	Derby	9·618	York, Co.	21·168	York, Co.	18·608	Northumb.	1572
Cumberland	16·508	Notts	13·015	York, Co.	2013	York, Co.	8·819	Northumb.	20·195	Derby	16·973	Westmreld.	1422
Northumb.	16·408	Surrey	12·842	Westmreld.	1541	Northumb.	8·751	Durham	18·962	Northumb.	15·443	York, Co.	1406
6 Manu. Cs.	15·094	Derby	11·541	Notts	1337	Notts	8·153	Monmouth	15·480	6 Manu. Cs.	14·856	Notts	1031
Surrey	13·389	York, Co.	11·288	Surrey	1308	22 Agri. Cs.	7·156	Cumberland	12·971	Notts	13·731	6 Manu. Cs.	803
Gloucester	12·545	Middlesex	10·964	6 Manu. Cs.	1194	Monmouth	6·634	Surrey	12·102	22 Agri. Cs.	10·865	Surrey	802
Middlesex	12·156	6 Manu. Cs.	10·282	22 Agri. Cs.	1077	6 Manu. Cs.	6·336	22 Agri.Cs.	11·433	Monmouth	8·154	22 Agri. Cs.	801
Durham	11·621	Monmouth	9·951	Monmouth	974	Surrey	3·884	Worcester	10·560	Worcester	8·096	Monmouth	753
22 Agri. Cs.	11·277	22 Agri.Cs.	9·858	Middlesex	818	Gloucester	3·370	6 Manu. Cs.	9·144	Middlesex	7·207	Worcester	540
Monmouth	10·715	Gloucester	9·609	Gloucester	776	Worcester	3·154	Gloucester	8·065	Surrey	7·070	Gloucester	538
Worcester	8·675	Worcester	4·048	Worcester	761	Middlesex	1·679	Middlesex	6·012	Gloucester	6·741	Middlesex	469
All England	12·839		10·440		1145		4·711		10·600		11·359		789

Remark on this Table need only be very brief. The position of the four northern mining, and agricultural counties, of Cornwall, of Yorkshire, and of Derby and Notts, is very striking. Under the 3rd, 4th, and 5th columns, these eight counties, though in a different order, respectively to each other, take precedence of all others. The only displacements of this order, are as respects Durham, under the 1st column, and a single break in the 3rd, 6th, and 7th columns. Exactly in the other extreme of the scale, stand Gloucester and Worcester, only less criminal than the metropolitan county. Other points of interest and value will so readily suggest themselves, that further observation on the Table is unnecessary.

SUMMARY OF THE CHAPTER.

THE question mooted in this chapter, namely, the comparative morality of the manufacturing and agricultural counties, has now received a sufficiently extended, minute, and, it is hoped, impartial investigation. In the selection of the counties compared, care has been taken to exclude such as presented extreme ratios of crime, either way, when accompanied by marked differences or peculiarities of social or industrial organization. The reasons for such exclusion have been given, in the course of investigation, and need not be repeated here. The actual ratio of the total criminality of each group has first been ascertained. That ratio has been corrected, for certain differences in the proportions of the population betwixt fifteen and thirty years of age, in conformity with the law so clearly developed by Mr. Neison; and a further correction has been made, to compensate for the excess of the operative and lower classes, in certain counties,—the ground of such compensation being the obvious fact, that those classes furnish the great mass of offenders brought before the local and the county tribunals. The period of time selected for this comparison is the year 1845, or rather, the average of 1844, 1845, and 1846. The selection of that period has been justified, because it was a period, on the whole, of good trade and fair employment, undisturbed by violent oscillation in the price of food,—which, as was shown to demonstration in the preceding chapter, greatly influences the amount of crime, and with a much more intense and violent action, in the manufacturing than the agricultural counties. The result shows a ratio of criminality, of 1 in 157, in the former group, and 1 in 137 in the latter. But these ratios need another correction,— namely, for the different proportions of the criminal class, specifically so called, in the respective groups; there being no question that the dense town and city populations of the great seats of industry, afford alike a place of refuge, and fields for the exercise of their predatory craft, to this *pariah* and exotic tribe. No exact analysis of crime can be obtained, until the exact proportion of this class to the indigenous and really working population of the respective groups, which is separate and distinct from what must be considered a foreign, or, if a new compound may be ventured, a non-indigenous body—is ascertained.

It would also be necessary to separate from the crime of each county that portion which is committed by the changing population of the sea-ports, which greatly affects the general average in several of the counties compared, and especially Lancashire, Southampton, and Devon. Only a few scattered data exist to guide the inquirer, and those not sufficiently extensive or definite to warrant a broad induction. They are adduced rather to point out the path to be explored, than as the basis of general conclusions. They are, nevertheless, extremely significant and suggestive. In brief, they are as follows :—

The criminal statistics of Manchester for 1849, contain a Table (No. 28) showing the "trade of all the prisoners taken into custody in 1849, and how they were disposed of by the magistrates." A very condensed abstract gives the following results :—

Number of persons apprehended in 1849   -   4687
Discharged   -   -   -   1726
Summarily convicted   -   2311
Committed for trial -   -   650

Classifying the summary convictions, and the committals to the Sessions and Assizes, according to the occupation of the prisoners, the following results are obtained :—

G

Class or Occupation.	Summarily convicted.	Ratio to Number of the Class. 1 in	Committed for Trial.	Ratio to Number of the Class. 1 in
Spinners, Weavers, Dyers, Fustian Cutters, &c.	305	147	105	428
Labourers - - - - -	302	20	80	76
Engineers, Mechanics, Smiths, Joiners, and Sawyers - - - -	181	96	48	98
Tailors & Shoemakers -	76	65	18	277
Masons, Bricklayers, Painters, &c. - - -	122	37	28	162
Butchers, Bakers, Brewers, and Publicans -	62	48	12	252
Coachmen, Carters, Porters, and Packers -	157	21	30	112
Servants and Charwomen	47	249	44	267
Clerks - - - - - -	30	168	21	97
All others - - - - -	194	27	49	109
Reputed Thieves - - -	131	2	74	4
Prostitutes - - - -	366	2	76	5
No Trade - - - - -	338	..	65	..
	2311	..	650	..
Average of all Manchester	..	130	..	464

Assuming 100 as representing the total of all the classes above enumerated,* the following Table will show the proportions of the above classes to that number, and the percentage of prisoners furnished by each class, to the total number of the summarily convicted and the tried.

* This number only includes the persons of all ages and both sexes actually engaged in the respective trades.

Proportion of Population.	CLASSES.	Proportion of Prisoners to Total of Summary Convictions.	Proportion of Prisoners to Total committed for Trial.
49·	Factory and Manufacturing Population- }	13·2	16·2
6·7	Labourers	13·1	12·3
5·2	Engineers, &c.	7·8	7·4
5·6	Tailors and Shoemakers	3·3	2·8
4·9	Masons, Bricklayers, &c.	5·2	4·3
3·3	Butchers, Bakers, &c.	2·6	1·8
3·7	Coachmen, &c.	6·8	4·6
13·	Servants	2·1	6·7
2·3	Clerks	1·7	3·2
5·	All others	8·2	7·5
98·7		64·	66·8
1·3	{ No trade	14·6	10·1
	{ Prostitutes	15·8	11·7
	{ Reputed Thieves	5·6	11·4
100		100	100

It appears from this analysis, that the really manufacturing section of the Manchester population, though constituting one-half of the whole, only commits one-sixth of the crime which is tried at the sessions and the assizes, and rather more than one-eighth of that which is summarily disposed of.   It is also shown, that the class of labourers, though little more than one-sixteenth of the population, and the various classes of handicrafts, constituting one-sixth of the population, each commit nearly as much crime as the manufacturing population: and that the really criminal

G 2

and profligate class, combined with the class having *no trade*, and who may be concluded to belong to one or other of the two last-named, commit *one-third* of all the crime in Manchester.

The whole result will appear more graphically thus :—

Percentage to Population.	CLASSES.	Percentage Summary Convictions.	Percentage committed for Trial.
49·	Manufacturing Classes -	13·2	16·2
6·7	Labourers - - - - -	13·1	12·3
43·0	{ Handicraftsmen, Retail Dealers, Servants, Clerks, &c. &c. }	37·7	37·3
1·3	No Trade, Prostitutes, &c.	36·0	33·2
100	... ...	100	100

The conclusion demonstrated by this short Table, combined with the two immediately preceding, cannot be better expressed than in the words of the Rev. John Clay, chaplain of the Preston House of Correction :—" It is now sufficiently evident, that it is not a manufacturing population, as such, which fosters crime. . . It is not manufacturing Manchester, but multitudinous Manchester, which gives birth to whatever criminality may be imputable to it. It is the *large town,* to which both idle profligates and practised villains resort, as a likely field for the indulgence of sensuality, or the prosecution of schemes of *plunder.*"

The criminal and police returns unfortunately do not supply the particulars of the trade and occupation of offenders of any other town except Hull, and that portion of the metropolis which is under the surveillance of the metropolitan police. The industrial economy of the metropolis is very different to that of Manchester, inasmuch as the former is essentially a mercantile depôt, the latter a manufacturing focus. Still, there are many points of analogy, and especially as respects the comparative criminality of the *labourers,* properly so called, and the proportion of the total of all offences committed by the specific criminal class. The Table following is a very condensed analysis of the returns of the metropolitan police district for 1842 and 1845, respectively :—

Metropolitan Police Returns.

Occupation.	1842. Percentage to Total Crime.	Total Crime.	1845. Percentage to Total Crime.	Total Crime.
Weavers, &c. - - - -	1·6	1·033	1·4	859
Labourers - - - - -	23·5	15·454	23·9	14·066
Engineers, Smiths, Joiners, &c., &c. - - - - -	3·7	2·467	2·1	1·269
Tailors and Shoemakers -	4·9	3·199	5·1	3·078
Masons, Bricklayers, Plasterers, Painters, &c. -	1·6	1·069	5·5	3·253
Butchers and Bakers - -	1·7	1·130	1·4	·845
Coachmen, Porters, &c. -	1·6	1·068	1·9	1·107
Servants, Charwomen, and Laundresses - - -	4·4	2·881	3·5	2·026
Clerks - - - - - -	·6	440	·9	531
Retail Traders - - - -	3·1	2·057	2·9	1·716
Other Handicraft Trades -	5·1	3·357	1·5	902
All other Persons - - -	1·8	1·144	3·9	2·305
Sailors - - - - - -	2·2	1·445	3·	1·805
Soldiers - - - - -	·6	366	·4	257
No Trade - - - - -	43·6	28·594	42·6	25·104
	100	65·704	100	59·123

Abstract of the Hull Police Return for 1849.

OFFENCES COMMITTED BY.	Number.	Percentage to Total Crime.
Factory Hands - - - - - -	93	3·4
Labourers - - - - - -	701	24·5
Engineers, Smiths, &c. - - -	110	3·8
Tailors and Shoemakers - - -	82	2·9
Masons and Bricklayers - - -	82	2·9
Butchers and Bakers - - - -	22	·8
Clerks - - - - - - -	11	·4
Retail Traders - - - - -	75	2·6
Other Handicrafts Tradesmen -	98	3·4
Sailors, Watermen and Fishermen	400	14·
Soldiers - - - - - - -	18	·7
All others - - - - - -	74	2·6
No Trade - - - - - -	1086	38·
	2862	100·0

There are many points of close and striking analogy betwixt this Table and the Manchester one, and more especially in the percentage of crime committed by *labourers*, and by the vagrant and predatory class. The former class,—labourers,—constitute a higher proportion in the manufacturing districts and in Middlesex, than in the agricultural districts, by nearly 2 per cent. The incidence of this excess on the amount of crime is not, however, to be measured by that numeral, but by the degree in which the criminality of the class, labourers, exceeds that of all other classes. Now this class in Manchester is only 6·7 per cent., or about one-fifteenth of the population of actual workers (excluding the *residue* of women and chil-

dren); but it furnishes *one-fifth of the crime.* The effect
on the total of offences in a county having 5 per cent.
more of the labourers, than another in all other respects
alike, would be to add 15 per cent. of crime, pro rata, to
the general average of the population. The criminality of
the class is not matter of surprise, seeing that it comprises the *least* skilled and educated of the operative
classes. Mere manual strength is the main requisite; and
thus the occupation absorbs all who have no capacity
for higher branches of employment.

But the distinctive and most important feature, common
to all these Tables, is the vast proportion of all the crime of
Manchester, Hull, and of the metropolitan district, committed by the disorderly and criminal classes; for there is
no question that the negative designation, " *No Trade,*"
on the Metropolitan and Hull Tables, points out the three
classes of criminals which in the Manchester Table are
designated respectively, " *reputed thieves,*" " *no trade,*"
and " *prostitutes.*" The proportions of crime, however,
differ in the two localities,—that of London exceeding
Manchester by about 8 per cent.;—the average of the
former being about 43 per cent. of the total crime, and of
the latter 35 per cent. These figures suggest a grave question,—one, in fact, on the solution of which most important conclusions depend. If 40 or even 30 per cent.
of the crime of the metropolis be committed by the criminal class, then, in whatever degree the crime so committed exceeds the crime perpetrated by the same class in
other counties, the crime of the metropolis will require
correction, in order to a fair comparison of the relative
morality of the indigenous and industrious classes.

What is the ratio of such offences in other counties?

There are no exact data on which to frame a reply. But conjecture is warrantable, and perhaps will not be far astray. Let it be supposed, then, that 30 per cent. of all the crime in the metropolitan county is committed by the criminal class, and that 10 per cent. is the proportion in Lincolnshire. Now, as the class under consideration constitutes but a small proportion of the total population, relatively to the number of offences committed by it, the actual ratio of the criminality of the other classes in each county would be ascertained by deducting from the total of crime in Middlesex 30 per cent., and from the total crime of Lincoln 10 per cent., dividing the population by the residue in each case. The actual ratios of crime in the two counties, for 1845, are 384 and 851, respectively. Corrected in the manner indicated, the ratios would be 548 and 923, respectively. The ratios represent the comparative morality of all the population apart from the criminal class, specifically so called, *or* of all the population apart from the specific criminal class. Before the correction, the crime of Lincolnshire was as 117 in each 100,000 of the population, after it, 108. In Middlesex, before the correction, it was 261 in 100,000, and after it, 182. Middlesex, then, instead of appearing to be 124 per cent. more criminal than Lincoln, would only show an excess of 74 per cent. The probability is, however, that the excess is considerably less even than that; and if allowance be made for the greater number and intensity of the motives and temptations to crime in Middlesex than in Lincoln, the morality of the two is not far from par,—so far as crime against the law of the land may be taken as a measure of morality. The morality of many districts, measured by this test, is in truth an imaginary quantity:

it only indicates the absence of the occasion, and the incentive to commit offences.

The effect of a large sea-faring population on the amount of crime is mournfully illustrated by the criminal statistics of Liverpool; though it must be noted, that the instance there is complicated by the very large proportion which Irish immigrants of the lowest class form of the whole population. The chaplain of Preston House of Correction has put the high criminality of Liverpool in a strong light, in a Table at page 15 of his Report for 1849. The Table shows, that in the four towns of Manchester,—Salford, Bolton, and Preston,—with a population of 489,000, there were 11,477 apprehensions, being 2·30 of the population; and in Liverpool, with a population of 299,000, there were 22·036 apprehensions, being 5·64 of the population! Analysing the totals, he shows that, whilst the population of Liverpool is *one-fifth* less than the towns named,

The commitments for trial are equal;

The apprehensions two-and-half times greater;

The females apprehended nearly three times as great;

The juveniles charged with felony nearly three times greater;

The summary convictions for all offences three-and-half times greater;

The summary convictions for robberies more than seventeen times greater.

The extraordinary fact last named accounts for the anomaly, that, whilst the apprehensions are two-and-half times greater, the committals for trial are equal. The fact is, that a vast number of robberies from sailors and others going abroad immediately, are disposed of summarily by the magistrates, which would otherwise go to

the sessions. There can be little doubt that crime in
Bristol, Portsmouth, Plymouth, and London, is similarly
increased by the presence of a large sea-faring population,
a class singularly reckless in their habits when ashore, and
exposed to the arts of the very lowest depredators, both
male and female. The crime of Liverpool is probably
greater than in any of the other ports, because of its greater
Irish population; since it appears, that of 6194 persons
brought before the magistrates of that town in 1849,
for felonies, 3266, or *more than one-half*, were natives
of Ireland, the Irish constituting one-fourth of the population. Even in Preston, the Irish immigrants constituted, in 1849, 54 per cent. of the summary convictions.
There is melancholy evidence indeed, that this class has
greatly increased in Lancashire and the West Riding of
York, during the last four years, (so fatal to Ireland), and
is eating like a canker into the social body. The calendars
proclaim the fact by the preponderance of Irish names.
The general opinion too is, that the class of immigrants
now reaching the English shore is the very lowest, physically, morally, and intellectually, ever cast upon it, by the
mortal throes of the sister island. The children especially,
have all that wild and bewildered air which characterizes
the young savage, when first brought into contact with the
forms and spectacles of civilized life; and so marked is
the repulsiveness of their whole physiognomy and aspect,—
so animal, and so *un*-intellectual, that, in the same mills,
the English juvenile operatives refuse to associate with
them. The habits of the entire class, juvenile and adult,
are filthy and revolting, and their turbulence a constant
source of annoyance to the peaceable and well-disposed,
and most costly, in the shape of police and gaol expendi-

ture, to the localities which are unhappily invaded by them.

The broad general conclusion from the preceding analysis is this : that there is a far larger proportion of all offences committed by the vagrant and predatory classes in the manufacturing than the agricultural counties, because of the greater number and populousness of the towns,—to which, for reasons sufficiently stated before, these dangerous and vicious classes resort. What that difference of proportion really is, remains a problem to be solved. It is palpably not a slight one, and it is, perhaps, not going beyond sober probability to say, that in Lancashire, and the West Riding of York and Warwickshire, the ratios of crime are aggravated by it, from a fifth to a *fourth*. If so, then the difference in the comparative moral condition of the manufacturing and agricultural counties is also far more in favour of the former, than is shown by the Table at page 7 ; but as that difference admits of no accurate measurement, it can only be stated in these general terms.

ON THE CONNEXION BETWIXT THE RETARD-ATION IN THE PROGRESS OF CRIME, FROM 1821 TO 1845, AS COMPARED WITH ITS PRO-GRESS FROM 1805 TO 1821, AND THE PRO-GRESS OF SUNDAY AND DAY-SCHOOL IN-STRUCTION.

It is presumed, that the fact of a great retardation in the progress of crime, betwixt 1821 and 1845, was completely proved in the second chapter. Assuming that to be admitted, it is proposed to place it in juxtaposition with *another fact*, namely, the simultaneous increase in the means of Sabbath and day-school education, and to detect what connexion, as cause and effect, or otherwise, there may be betwixt them. The evidence of that other fact, it is scarcely necessary to say, rests on the statistics of Mr. Baines, as developed in his letter to Lord John Russell during the controversy on national education,—supported and confirmed by the inquiry and conclusions of Charles Knight and Professor Hoppus, at a subsequent period. If the absence of all reply in the way of refutation, entitled to a moment's consideration, can be taken as evidence of truth, these statistics bear its stamp,—for they are un-answered. If answer could have been found, no question exists that it would have been given to the world. It does not from this logically follow that Mr. Baines' statistics are unanswerable, — but it does establish a probability so strong, that no hesitation is felt in reasoning upon them as demonstrated quantities.

The following Tables place the two facts in juxta-position :—

Years.	Scholars.	Population.	Proportion of Day Scholars to Population.
1803	524·241	9·128·597	1 in 17½
1818	674·883	11·398·167	1 in 17
1833	1·276·847	14·417·110	1 in 11½
1846	2·000·000	17·026·024	1 in 8½

Criminals in 100,000.		Increase in the Ratio of Crime, relatively to Population, from 1801 to 1845.	
1801	- - 54 - -	1801 to 1821 -	112 per cent.
1821	- - 115 - -	1821 to 1831 -	26·9 ,,
1831	- - 146 - -	1831 to 1845 -	6·9 ,,
1845	- - 156		

These Tables show, that, concurrently with a vast aug-mentation of the instruction given to the people of England and Wales (for it must be especially noted that the in-crease of scholars betwixt 1833 and 1818, and again, betwixt 1833 and 1846, would be mainly of the operative classes), there has been a corresponding retardation in the progress of *crime.* Is the concurrence simple,—or con-sequential? Are both phenomena results of a common antecedent,—or, is the one just the direct effect of the other? In other words,—is crime stayed in its onward pro-gress, because education is extending and counteracting it?

It will greatly assist to determine this problem, if it can be shown that the changes which have taken place in the social and industrial condition of England and Wales, during the period under review, have been just of that kind which have rendered more active all the temptations and facilities to crime. Now if one fact lies more upon

the surface of society than another, with reference to
crime, it is, that dense town populations greatly augment
it, and especially town populations in which the more
opulent classes, whether tradesmen, merchants, or manufacturers, constitute a large proportion of the whole.
Great wealth in juxtaposition with large aggregations of
people, are precisely the two conditions in which, other
things being alike, crime will be most rife.   The changes
which have taken place in England since 1801, have been
precisely of the kind to realize these conditions in all the
manufacturing, the mining, and the metropolitan counties,
in a very high degree, and in a less degree in the agricultural counties.   The progress of the population betwixt
1801 and 1845 is without any parallel in the history of
England, being considerably more than double that of the
entire preceding century.   Dividing the counties, as before,
the relative progress of population in each section is as
follows :—

	Population, 1801.	Population, 1845.	Increase per Cent.
22 Agricultural Counties	3,835,280	5,792,789	51·
6 Manufacturing ditto	2,007,188	5,163,195	157·2
3 Mining { Durham Cornwall Monmouth	394,212	859,303	118·
2 Metro- politan counties { Middlesex and Surrey	1,087,172	2,308,842	102·4
7 other Counties - -	1,007,582	1,745,156	73·2
40 All England - -	8,331,434	15,869,285	90·5

Here is overwhelming evidence, that in the seats of manufactures, the increase in the density of the population has been exceedingly great, that increase being not far short of double the ratio of the increase of all England, and more than threefold the increase of the agricultural counties. In the mining and metropolitan counties also, the increase is very large. That the increase in the manufacturing counties has been chiefly in the *towns*, is made equally evident by the following Table :—

	Town Population, 1801.	Town Population, 1841.	Increase, 1801 to 1841.
Lancashire 11 Towns	296,780	941,189	317 per cent.
Warwick 2 ditto	89,704	213,665	137 ditto
Yorksh.W.R. 6 ditto	115,154	314,323	173 ditto
Cheshire 4 ditto	40,362	98,077	145 ditto
Stafford 4 ditto	45,065	129,697	189 ditto
	587,065	1,696,931	
Supposed increase 1841 to 1845		169,693	
		1,866,624	217

Vast as is this increase of the town population, it is exclusive of the small towns, under 20,000 inhabitants, in which manufacturing industry has concentrated in the six counties under consideration, and more especially in South Lancashire, the West Riding of York, and Cheshire. A very cursory glance at the Population Tables, shows that the small towns of the kind alluded to, contain upwards of one million of inhabitants,—so that considerably more than *one half* the population of six manufacturing counties is exclusively engaged in various branches of manufacturing art, and congregated in dense masses, from 2000 or 3000, to 300,000 in number.

As the consequence of the growth of manufactures, wealth in every form has accumulated, and that in a degree more than commensurate with the growth of the population. If any reliance can be placed on the statements of public writers, and more especially of Arthur Young, the rental of real property has increased upwards of 250 per cent. within the last eighty years, and there can be no doubt that the personal property of the nation has increased still more largely. The materials for exact conclusion do not exist, but there is one authentic public document, bearing upon this point, of great significance, namely—the returns of real property charged to the Income Tax in 1815 and 1843 respectively. A condensed abstract of this valuable document gives the following results :—

Real Property charged to the Income Tax.

COUNTIES.	1815.	1843.	Increase per Cent.
	£	£	
6 Manufacturing Counties, including West Riding of York - -	9,852,493	20,179,893	104·8
22 Agricultural Counties, including North and East Ridings of York - - - - -	24,582,910	35,543,072	44·5
3 Mining Counties - -	2,002,516	3,613,107	80·8
2 Metropolitan Counties -	7,174,710	14,294,917	99·2
7 other Counties - - -	6,131,993	8,715,710	42·1
	49,744,622	82,346,699	65·8

The increase of the total population of England in the forty years betwixt 1801 and 1845, has been stated at page 134 as 90·5 per cent. The period embraced by the two returns under the Income Tax, comprises twenty-eight years, and the increase of the population during that period would be about 54 per cent. The preceding return, therefore, shows that real property has advanced more rapidly than population, the increase for all England being 65 per cent. In fact, the increase of real property in all the five divisions of counties, betwixt 1815 and 1843, was greater than the increase of population, but the excess was comparatively small in the agricultural and other counties. In the metropolitan and manufacturing counties, the excess was nearly 30 per cent., as compared with the increase of the population. It is obvious, too, that whilst in the agricultural districts, any increase in the value of real property would not necessarily involve a corresponding increase of personal or moveable property ; in the metropolitan and manufacturing counties, the increase of the latter kind of property would necessarily be augmented, and probably in a greater degree. Indeed, the more rapid increase of real property in the manufacturing than in the agricultural counties, has just been, because of the growth of all the other kinds of property there. It is out of the profits of trade and manufactures that the immense aggregation of real property in the shape of mills, docks, railways, houses, &c., has taken place in the two great counties of Lancashire and the West Riding of York; and to this cause is the greatly augmented rental of land owing—the accumulation of manufacturing profit acting upon rent in two ways—first, by increasing the demand for land for building and other purposes—and second, by a more active demand for all kinds of agricultural produce, a demand the most intense in the immediate neighbourhood of the greatest aggregations of the population.

The social condition of the manufacturing districts, betwixt 1821 and 1845, may be described as one in which the temptations and facilities to commit crimes against property have been greatly augmented, as well as the means of concealment or harbourage for the predatory and dangerous classes of society. The whole structure of society has tended to multiply the seductions which assail the middle and upper classes, and the good things, which tempt the honesty of the more dependent operative classes. The resort of the vicious classes to the secluded lanes and courts of the large towns, has multiplied the corrupting influences, always rife in the midst of wealth and luxury, whilst the isolation of the operative classes, in great masses, from the other ranks of society, has tended to weaken those good moral influences, which, descending from the upper stratum of society, permeate all below. Yet, in spite of all these unfavourable conditions, the progress of crime in these counties has received a mighty check, as the following statements will show :—

COUNTY.	Increase in the Ratio of Crime to Population, 1821 on 1801.	Increase in the Ratio of Crime to Population, 1831 on 1821.	Increase in the Ratio of Crime to Population, 1845 on 1831.	——
			Increase.	Decrease.
Chester - -	177½	38·	9·3	...
Lancaster -	270	2·6	...	6·4
Leicester -	170	11·6	63·	...
Stafford - -	180	46·6	...	5·4
Warwick -	105	4·	Par.	...
York - -	160	42·6	...	6·2
Middlesex -	113	5·2	...	8·6
All England	115	26·9	...	6·9

It was observed, in commenting upon the extraordinary and rapid increase of crime betwixt 1801 and 1821, and more especially subsequently to 1814, that there must have been some alterations of the law, whereby *new offences* were created, which transferred to the sessions and assizes, offences previously disposed of in a summary manner ; and therefore, that, in all probability, the increase was, to a considerable extent, apparent only. But it is quite incredible that any alterations in the law can account for the entire difference shown above. Even were the figures in the first column reduced one half, the augmentation of crime, betwixt 1801 and 1821, compared with its progress in the two following periods of ten and fifteen years respectively, incontestably shows that some moral element was operative, in the latter cycles, so mighty as not merely to arrest the further progress of crime, but actually to drive back the flood, which all the surrounding elements conspired to *swell*.

And this fact must be especially noted in estimating the force of the surrounding element. That portion of all crime which is committed by the dangerous—the criminal class—must have been on the increase, relatively to the population, throughout the whole period under review, in the densely crowded seats of manufacture. If, then, *all* crime is stationary, or diminishing, relatively to the entire population, it is a necessary sequence, that all other classes, apart from the criminal class, *per se*, are less criminal than *heretofore*, the degree of diminution in their criminality being exactly correspondent to the increase of the offences committed by the dangerous classes.

Here, then, is a striking and undeniable moral result—diminished infraction of the laws; for it is assumed that, in a greater or less degree, all infraction of the laws is a breach of some moral obligation. Now the nature of a cause may be safely inferred from the effect. Thistles do not yield grapes, nor thorns, figs! Moral effects must have moral causes. Where is that moral cause to be found, which has produced such happy effects in the manufacturing districts, except it be in sabbath and day-school instruction? No hesitation will be felt in giving an affirmative answer, by those who are cognizant of the many forms in which the good fruits of that instruction have manifested themselves, besides in the repression of offences against the public laws of the community. The fruits have been positive as well as negative. There is an unmistakeable softening of the public manners. There is an increased desire for intellectual improvement, clearly manifested in the spread of Mechanics' Institutes, Libraries, and Youth's Guardian Societies. Disputes betwixt the different sections of society, on the existing questions of the day,—WAGES AND LABOUR'S RIGHTS,—are conducted with better temper, and the appeal is made to broader and more benevolent principles than heretofore ; and the relationships of employer and employed rest on a more generous and candid estimate, each of the other!

It may be,—and the conjecture is not vaguely or hesitatingly put,—that the very closeness of the several classes, in large towns, has combined, with the spread of education, to secure these results. True, there is apparently a wider gulf between the *capitalist and the labourer*, than under the olden, the domestic system ; but then there is compensation for that in the unquestioned intellectual and moral superiority, in the main, of the great capitalists of the present day, over the domestic manufacturers of the last and preceding generations. The employer now, can do far more than the employer of the last century, to advance the intellectual and moral well-being of the employed. The very concentration of the masses is favourable to concentration in the means employed, and all that is gained in concentration is a gain of power. The factory system, too, in itself, has a powerful direct influence on the character of the operative. It is essentially a system of method, order, and co-operation. It requires corresponding qualities and habits in the operative. It is a gross, vulgar error, to suppose that the factory operative is a mere machine—devoid of intelligence. He must comprehend the machine which he guides or watches, the nature of the processes which the *material* it acts upon undergoes, and he must harmoniously and cheerfully club his aid, and combine it with the aggregate labour of his fellows. Hence his frankness and manly good humour. The factory system, too, enforces sobriety, at least during the hours of labour.

An intemperate factory operative will at least receive no countenance for his intemperance, whilst at his work;— he will not, in fact, be endured. It only needs that general opinion should be more ripe, as to the obligations of employers to consider the moral claims of their work-people upon them, and the establishment of a broad basis of mutual respect and kindly feeling betwixt employers and employed, (simply as the result of the full recognition of their obligations by the former), to constitute the factory system one of the most powerful means, next to the offices of religious teaching, of raising the intellectual and moral character of the entire people in the manu-facturing districts. The system has borne good fruits already, but they are only the first fruits—the harvest is yet to be reaped.

Is it, then, unwarrantable to conclude that the retard-ation of crime in general, and its actual diminution in several conspicuous and striking instances, is owing to the spread of sabbath and day-school instruction? It is thought not — nay, it seems the only solution of the phenomena. Let it not be supposed, however, that such instruction alone has produced the results detailed. The spread of education is only one of many results, having a common origin or cause. It is undeniable that the middle classes of the large towns have brought, year by year, a more enlarged intelligence, a warmer philanthropy, and a deeper feeling of religious obligation, to bear, in all efforts to raise the classes below them, both intellectually and morally. They have sustained the sabbath-school system, and they have sustained, in by far the largest degree, the day-school effort. But it is not in these forms of effort only, that their intelligent benevolence has been operative. In a thousand other forms, and through a thousand other channels, a beneficent and holy influence has been exercised; and it is believed, that, so far from the efforts of the class having reached their climax, they are daily becoming more extended, and as they extend, are more wisely adapted to secure their great end. Happy will it be, when,.as the result of their efforts, those whose good they seek become fully alive to the value of what is offered to them, and meet the hand that holds it out, with the earnestness of men who see in it the alone means of social advancement, of a wise and safe liberty, and of true personal happiness.

THE CRIMINAL CLASS.

I# the investigation of the character and progress of crime, up to this point, has been correctly conducted, the fact is rendered all but certain, that the rapid growth of the population, and its aggregation in large and dense masses in the towns and cities òf England, has been accompanied with a corresponding, or perhaps larger growth of the criminal or dangerous classes. Under this designation, it may be as well to state at once, are included not only the professional thief or burglar, but the whole rabble of the vagrant and dissolute classes, who labour by fits, and eke out subsistence by pilfering, and who are ever on the verge of a more serious breach of the laws. No means exist of determining the rate of increase, or otherwise, in these classes, relatively to the population, prior to 1839; but the evidence that the number is considerable is abundant, a portion of that evidence having already been given in the condensed abstract of the Metropolitan, the Manchester, and the Hull Police Reports. These show that the proportion of the offences committed in those places by the vicious and dangerous classes combined, are respectively 33, 38, and 43 per cent. to the total number of offences. It is a legitimate conclusion, that the returns for all towns of like organization would exhibit similar proportions; and it is perhaps a safe conclusion, that one-third of the criminality of the *large* town population is traceable to these classes. This estimate is strengthened by the returns of summary convictions, from which it

appears, that on the average of the eight years extending
from 1839 to 1846, the mean proportion of the offences
committed by the two classes,—" vagrants and reputed
thieves,"—to the total of convictions, was 35·4 per cent. ;
and it must be noted, that this was the proportion, not for
the towns simply, but for all ENGLAND AND WALES.

Assuming, then, *one-third* of all town offences, cognizable
at the sessions and assizes, to be committed by the criminal
class, it may not be impracticable to arrive at a calculation
of the absolute number of such offences, which may be
tolerably proximate to the real number. The total population of the towns in England, containing 14,000 and
upwards, is more than five millions, say one-third of the
total population. The annual mean of offences tried at
the sessions and assizes betwixt 1839 and 1846, was
27·120. One-third of that number is 9·040 ; but as crime
is more rife in the towns than elsewhere, perhaps 10·500
is under rather than over the number of offences committed
by the town population. One-third of that number gives
3·500 as the total of offences committed by the criminal
class, or 12·9 per cent. of all offences committed in England and Wales. To this must be added another amount,
which can only be conjectured, namely, the proportion of
offences committed by the criminal class in all other parts
of England, apart from the large towns. Hazarding the
supposition that 10 per cent. does not exceed that proportion, it follows that 5162 represents the total of offences
committed by that class, or 19 per cent. of the total of
offences betwixt 1839 and 1846. The evil is one, then, of
great magnitude. It does not, however, convey a definite
idea to the mind, simply to put the proposition that a certain
class of the population commits one-fifth of all the crime of

H

the country. To attain that idea, it is necessary to estimate the pecuniary cost and the social evils of the crime
committed by the class. The first is perhaps not less than
£500,000 per annum expended on police and prisons, and the
administration of the law. But the cost stops not here. The
criminal class live by depredation on all other classes. In
the main, their daily subsistence is so much lawlessly abstracted from the earnings of the industrious members of
society. They contribute nothing to the common stock,
but they must take something out of it. How much they
thus take, cannot be accurately ascertained in the present
state of knowledge as to the number of the class ; but
there can be little doubt it is a much larger sum than that
expended on the protection of property, and the punishment of offences against it. But the pecuniary evil is
light and insignificant, compared with the moral. The
criminal class live amongst, and are dove-tailed in, so to
speak, with the operative classes, whereby they constitute
so many points of vicious contact with those classes—so
many ducts by which the virus of a moral poison circulates
through and around them. They constitute a pestiferous
canker in the heart of every locality where they congregate, offending the sight, revolting the sensibilities, and
lowering, more or less, the moral status of all who come
into contact with them. Their very presence, and the
daily commission of offences by them, is an evil ; because
it so habituates society to the loathsome spectacle of the
one, and the constant *recurrence* of the other, that the
sensibilities become blunted, and the judgment benumbed
and stupified. Those who doubt that such are the results
need only try the effect of a brief survey of the purlieus of
St. Giles, for the first time, and compare their own im-

pression and feelings with those of some parochial officer, habituated to the sights and sounds there, and they will doubt no longer. Inflicting great evils on society, it is not surprising that speculation has been busy on the question of the origin and natural history of the criminal class; and probably on no social question has so much been said and written within the last ten years as on this. Hypothesis after hypothesis has been framed to account for the hideous phenomenon; but each has exemplified one or other, or all those sources of fallacy in the investigation of statistics, which Quetelet so well defines—" 1st, Having preconceived notions of the final result—2nd, neglecting the numbers which contradict the result wished for—or, 3rd, incompletely enumerating causes, and only attributing to one cause what belongs to a concurrence of many."

It is not intended to incur the charge of perpetrating any one of these fallacies by launching another hypothesis. The subject is intricate and involved, and no skilful hand has succeeded hitherto, either in an exact portraiture of the class, or in detecting one or more of the master causes of its existence and growth. The question, *how* the class sprung up, is a complex question of Game Laws, Poor Laws, Vagrant Acts, Prison Discipline (or *no* Discipline), Protection Laws, Bad Harvests, Isolation of Classes, and defective Education; and he who shall either assign to each of these sources its proper influence in creating the class, or develop the one element in the condition of the operative class, to which all other deteriorating causes are but subordinate, and, in fact, have no efficiency without it, will confer a lasting benefit on society. The task is as yet to be executed.

But whilst disclaiming all pretensions to develop the

H 2

theory of a criminal class, something may be done to clear away *the mistakes and fallacies* which have greatly helped to keep that theory in the category of unknown things; and in attempting to do this very briefly, no apology is offered for disposing of some fallacies, which lie in the way of a correct induction, in a summary manner.

The Criminal class is *not* the product of the factory system. The evidence of Captain Willis, Superintendent of the Manchester Police, and the Police returns of that borough, are decisive on this point; equally clear is the testimony of the Chaplain of *Preston Gaol*. It is not denied that the factory system, the efficient causes of which have been improvements in mechanical and chemical science, leading to the super-addition of steam power and machinery to manual strength and skill, has necessitated a vast aggregation of population within the narrow limits of towns, and thereby provided the two conditions necessary to the existence of a criminal class—plenty of plunder, and room for concealment. But the criminal classes do not therefore spring out of the manufacturing system, nor are they, in the main, drafted from the ranks of the factory operatives. " It is not,"—to repeat Mr. Clay's emphatic words,—" manufacturing Manchester, but multitudinous Manchester, which engenders crime." Against all this personal and statistical evidence, to which may be added the low ratio of crime in the West Riding of York, it is a mere rhetorical flourish, nothing more, to attribute the growth of crime, or crime in general, " to the newly-born manufacturing communities which have grown up apart from the sympathies of civilization." Neither does the criminal class originate in the want of proper sanitary regu-

lations, or the crowded and promiscuous condition of the
population of the *bye-lanes* and courts of the great towns.
The action of these conditions on the morals of the un-
happy class who are subjected to them, is unquestionably
most deteriorating; but the conditions themselves are
concomitants, not causes, of the moral debasement of that
class. To attribute the existence of the class to these evil
conditions of it, is akin to the cosmogony which places
the earth on a tortoise, but fails to say on what the tortoise
rests. All such hypotheses stop short of the master cause.

Still less is absolute want, or the deficiency of the means
of employment, the one efficient cause of the criminal
class. No question exists, that periods of distress, when
the means of employment are inadequate, greatly add to the
criminal class; but the additions are chiefly, if *not entirely*,
made by the abstraction of the more idle and dissolute of
the working classes, who waste all their evenings in good
times in vicious indulgence, and have therefore no resource
in periods of depression, but either to beg or steal. The
subsistence of the entire class is unlawfully abstracted,
either by fraud or force, from all other classes. Whatever
its amount, to that extent the other classes had the means
of purchasing commodities, or of setting labour directly
to work. It is generally believed that the property stolen
by the criminal classes, or got by fraud and begging, considerably exceeds per head the average wages of the working classes. Be that so or not, it is evident that if the
whole class ceased begging, and commenced working, the
means of purchasing what they produce would be just that
fund which they now filch away from the industrious and
the virtuous. The gain would be two-fold. An equi-
valent would be given for that which is now unlawfully

abstracted, and the cost of police and gaols would be reduced in proportion to the diminution of the criminal
class.

Last of all, it is not the total absence, or the bad quality
of education, which engenders the criminal class,—if by
education be understood the best scholastic instruction
applicable to the operative classes. That such an education would remove all crime, and destroy the criminal
class, is an every-day assertion, and it involves a fallacy so
erroneous and dangerous, that no excuse need be offered
for giving to it a fuller exposition than the other fallacies
or mistakes already touched upon.

The assertion involves the proposition, that a certain
amount of school instruction, intellectual and moral, is a
specific remedy for crime. It needs no logical acuteness
to detect the *fallacy here*,—it is just that of assigning to
one cause what belongs to a concurrence of causes. It is
seen that, in the middle classes, who can command that
certain amount of *school instruction*, and amongst sections
of the operative classes who have had corresponding advantages, crime is rare, — is the exception, and not the
rule; and *therefore* it is concluded education has done it
—the scholastic education, as distinguished from all other
influences. It is forgotten that the fact of such an education being given, implies other facts infinitely more important to the matter of training up a moral generation,
and annihilating crime, than mere scholastic instruction—
those facts being, the holy influences of the domestic
hearth and household, the example of parents and asso-
ciates, and in the greater number of instances, a spiritual
religious teaching. No one, at all acquainted with the
condition and character of the schools in this country for

the middle class, will doubt for a moment that the high morality of the class is attributable vastly more to the influence just named, than to scholastic training. Now, the instruction contended for by those who hold scholastic education to be a panacea for all moral ills, will not secure these influences. It is in fact just because they *are not*, that there is no scholastic education ;—and supposing the education to be, by means external to the class, superadded or forced upon it—the want of those influences would neutralize it. The almost absolute impotence of any possible education, which left all other conditions and circumstances of the class untouched, would then be seen and felt ; and the absurdity and folly of looking for direct moral results from mere intellectual culture, or from that culture combined with the best moral training which the school admits of, would soon be demonstrated. The school influences would be sorry counteractives to the influences of the courts and alleys, and almost *unknown lands* of our great towns and cities—the filth, the squalor, the obscenity, the blasphemy, and withal, the palpable antagonism of feeling and interest to all the world, of which the mark is on every forehead, and the bitter rancour in every heart. The connexion of the young criminal with his class must be broken, *ere* scholastic instruction could be made to tell on his moral nature. Such instruction would fall upon him as powerless and futile as straw darts on the scales of Leviathan, so long as the associations and the scenes of his daily domestic life, if domestic it may be called, bring daily, more than counteraction./ It would go far more to prove the assertion combated, if it could be shown that the criminal class consists of individuals, either themselves thrown off from the ranks of the virtuous and industrious,

because of crime originating in the ignorance or the bad
quality of education, or descended from those who were
so cast off.   Such proof would be pertinent and conclusive.
But is it so?   Is morality, or so much of morality as will
ensure obedience to social laws at least, a necessary consequence of a certain amount and quality of scholastic
instruction?   Or, is it true that the absence of that *certain
amount*, and the presence of immorality, are respectively,
cause and effect? or more correctly speaking, that the latter
is a consequence of the former, as darkness is of the absence
of light?   If this were so, then virtue would be an impossible thing in the absence of school instruction.   *Given,*
a people that had *no schools*, and there will be a people
without goodness or virtue!   Does any sane man believe
this, who knows what was the condition of England for
generations and centuries when reading and writing were
the accomplishments of the few?   It would be idle formally
to refute such a proposition.   Suffice it to say, that there
were warm hearts and noble natures, and the whole exhi-
bition of household and public virtue, when Englishmen, as
a people, were as unlettered as the lowest operative *now*.
The truth is, the advocates of scholastic education reason
as if reading and writing, and the intellectual training of
the schools, constituted the essence of the education which
forms the mental and moral character, instead of being a
mere appliance of education, properly so called.   The living
voice, the personal example, the oral and traditionary morality and knowledge of a people, the faculty of observation
of men and things, and the power of reflection, are all independent of the power to read or write, and are efficient to
make, and have made, many a noble character and many a
noble people ; and even where scholastic training is at its

best, the education which the boy and the man gets out of the school, has far more to do with the formation of his mind and character than what he gets in it. Well is it when both harmonize, and are adapted each to the other ; but to ignore all other intellectual and moral influences or education, just to bolster up the absurd crotchet that scholastic influence or education is all in all, is of that class of fallacies, of which the Tenterden Steeple and Goodwin Sands fallacy is simply an extravagant type.

But the whole theory of a criminal class may be looked at from an entirely different point of view. The class has been regarded hitherto, either as a sequence of errors in the frame and working of social institutions, or as a moral cesspool, into which all the offscourings and dregs of the community settle down and corrupt. Is there not a fundamental error involved in this view? May it not be said of the class that it is *in* the community, but neither *of* it, nor *from* it? Is it not the fact that a large majority of the class is so by descent, and stands as completely isolated from the other classes, in blood, in sympathies, in its domestic and social organization (if such terms are applicable to its conditions and institutions), as it is hostile to them in the whole "*ways and means*" of its temporal existence? If this view be correct in any great degree, is it not wide of the subject to seek for its source, either positively in the direct action of the social institutions which surround it, or negatively, in the deficiencies and omissions of those institutions? And further, should not all means for the repression, or if it be practicable, the extinction of the class, comprise, in addition to such elementary and moral training for the young as may be applicable, a far more comprehensive scheme of appliances,

H 3

sanitary, municipal, judicial, and above all, the direct
action of benevolent Christian efforts—the combined effect
of which shall be to hedge up the way of crime, to hold
up distinctly and palpably the advantages and sweets of
industry and honesty; and more than all, to forge afresh
the broken links of social sympathy, and to establish in
the hearts of the outcast race the feeling of common brother-
hood with those, towards whom their only aspect and
feeling now, is either alienation or hatred?

The realization of such a scheme may seem to some
utterly impracticable, and the very idea Utopian. Be that
so,—then, if educational appliances to the young will not
gradually dry up the class, by a process of moral ab-
sorption into the healthful portions of society, where is
the remedy for the curse?

It may be said, that the class is in a considerable part
fed from without. It is not denied that such is the fact.
All the physical and moral conditions of the class are so at
war with nature, that its mere perpetuation, as distinct
from its actual increase, would seem to be not simply
anomalous, but impossible. If this be so, then the question of education comes up again. It will be said,
the external supplies may be cut off. That would narrow
the solution of the problem, how to extinguish the class,
to a question of the application of the right moral means,
and of time. But will any possible perfection of human
institutions, political, social, or moral, destroy crime—or
rather, render the existence of a distinct criminal class
impossible? It will help to answer the question, if
the results of education amongst the middle and upper
classes be examined. It is almost inconceivable that the
mass of society should ever realize a condition, in all

respects so favourable to moral health, as that of the middle and upper classes of society. It is clear, however, that if such a consummation were practicable, it would be irrational to expect from it better fruits than it now bears. Well, then, is there no foul stain on those classes? Amongst that class which has been educated in the Halls of Oxford and Cambridge, and the classic schools of Eton and Harrow, is seduction an unpractised villany? Does it furnish no supplies to the unprincipled gamblers of the turf and the betting-room? Is the public purse, or the purse of the private tradesman, never touched dishonestly, by other than plebeian hands? Turning to the middle classes,—do the Insolvent and the Bankruptcy Courts, and the Court of Exchequer, furnish no instances of dishonesty in the dealings betwixt man and man, and betwixt man and the community? Are fraudulent debtors, and the defrauders of the Customs and Excise, and receivers of stolen goods, unknown classes amongst the intellectually and morally trained of the middle class? It were idle to pursue the questioning. The fact, that the best appliances fail in numerous instances, is stereotyped in all the past history of man, and is patented on the face of every society. Let it be attributed, by the astute theologian, to the natural depravity of man's nature, or by the dreamy stickler for the possible perfection of man, to a wrong application of means,—the sad and melancholy fact stands out as palpable and as enduring as the pyramids on the sandy plain of Jizeh, that each distinct class has its distinct phases and forms of vice and criminality,—but all agreeing in one sad particular, that, various as are their shapes, the essential moral turpitude of them is alike and equal.

If this be so, then the case may be put most strongly thus :—Let it be supposed that the entire criminal class were swept away—absorbed—annihilated—no matter how. Further, that the most approved intellectual and moral means were made applicable to all classes—would a criminal class be an impossibility? Different men, according to their views of human nature, or their theories of moral influence, will give different answers : but it does seem a conclusion unwarranted by all the experience of communities, and by all the light which ages have thrown on man's nature, in the infinite variety of position and circumstance of his being, that the class should ever cease out of the land. Every section of society has its intractables and incorrigibles,—those on whom moral appliances have failed, who are either cast out by society itself, or isolate themselves because they are in all parts of their nature antagonistic to it; and such of the humble operative classes as fall below that moral standard of their grade in society, which is the basis of admission to its privileges and friendships, are necessarily thrown off, and, as they can fall no lower, constitute a class apart,— "their hand against every man, and every man's hand against them."

Be these speculations correct or not, it will not be maintained by any one, who has deeply considered this complex question, to be irrelevant or profitless. The existence and the numbers of the criminal class is a great evil, and, it may be, a great and grave error on the part of society at large. How it is engendered—what are its elements—must be of permanent importance to be known. The first step to the effectual correction, or the greatest possible mitigation of this great evil,—and no less calamity,—will be the

recording with more accuracy and minuteness whatever
information can be elicited respecting the criminals who
pass through our courts of justice. More would be known,
after five years of careful scrutiny into the previous history
of our criminals, than will be got by fifty years of the
superficial and desultory observation which is at present
practised. The inquiry should extend to the place of birth,
occupation, place of residence, and to education, and other
moral influences ; in one word, all that is comprehended
in the phrase—the " Natural History" of the class. The
philosophy or theory of a criminal class, will assume a
tangible shape when that is accomplished, but not before :
and as, until the true theory be known, so neither can the
true remedy be known, the nation may lay its account in
the expenditure of a vast amount of money, on schemes of
prison discipline, and penal infliction, and industrial schools,
and national education—only to arrive at the conclusion
at last, that it has applied remedies without an accurate
knowledge of the disease, and has therefore acted the part
of the empiric or the quack, to the disgrace of its philosophy and its statesmanship.

JUVENILE CRIME.

ANY notice of the progress and character of crime would be incomplete, which did not touch upon the subject of juvenile crime. It would be a most painful fact—if fact at all—that juvenile crime is increasing. If the fountain be poisoned, what must the stream be? The supposition that such is the fact would go far, not simply to show the insufficiency of the increased Sunday and day-school education now given,—comparing the period from 1830 to 1850 with that from 1800 to 1830,—but would actually raise the question, whether the unquestioned progress in the quantum of education has not been actually mischievous. For to this, proof of an absolute increase in the ratio of juvenile offences must lead. The absolute and relative amount of education have both increased. The absolute and relative amount of juvenile crime have both increased. This is the case put. What is the direct, inevitable, and undeniable inference? Why, that education is either mischievous or inoperative. But those who affirm

that juvenile crime is increasing, deny both conclusions;
and he would be a bold man who should affirm, that the
Sunday and day-school instruction of the last twenty
years was not, in all respects, superior to that of the thirty
preceding years. The suspicion arises, that there is some
mistake or error in putting the case, or some flaw in the
reasoning from it. A little investigation will, perhaps,
warrant the affirmation, which is put without hesitancy,
that such suspicion is correct.

At page 9 of the Rev. Mr. Worsley's Essay on Juvenile
Depravity, he gives the proportion of the offences committed by juveniles under 20 years of age, to the total of
offences in each year, from 1842 to 1846 ; and concludes,
from the figures, that juvenile crime is greatly on the
increase.

	1842.	1843.	1844.	1845.	1846.
Aged under 15 years,	5·3	5·7	6·0	6·4	6·5
15 and under 20 years,	22·0	22·7	23·3	24·1	24·5

Now, it may startle Mr. Worsley to affirm, that this Table
proves nothing to the purpose. It does not prove an
absolute or even *relative* increase of juvenile crime as
respects the population; it only proves that, in the years
named, the proportion of juvenile *to all other* crimes
was steadily increasing. It might be the case, for aught
the figures show, that *all crime* was diminishing, but
juvenile crime, less than all other crimes. This is easily
proved. Taking the extreme years of the series, the total
of all crime, and of juvenile crime, for England and
Wales, was as follows :—

Total crime, 1842 - - 30,788   1846 - - 24,517
Juvenile crime, ,, - - 8,432   ,, - - 7,610

It must be noted that 1842 was the culminating point of crime in the disastrous period from 1839 to 1843. During that period *adult* crime was rife. Burglaries, highway robberies, and seditious offences, abounded, as is shown elsewhere; and hence the small proportion of juvenile crime. Now, population was at least 5 per cent. more in 1846 than in 1842. If so, the number of juvenile offences in 1846 should have been 8843. It was 7610, or less by 14 per cent. ! But further analysis shows, that in all England, except Middlesex, the absolute and relative decrease of juvenile crime was more than 14 per cent. The respective numbers of *all* offences, and of juvenile offences, in Middlesex, in 1842, was 4094 and 1350; and in 1846, 5175 and 1696. Deducting the juvenile offences, then, of Middlesex from those of all England for each year, the case would stand thus :—

Juvenile offences, 1842 - - 7082   1846 - - 5914

If juvenile crime had increased relatively to population, then the number of juvenile offences should have been 7436 ; but it was 5914, or less by 20 per cent., for all England, except Middlesex, than in 1842. Mr. Worsley's entire Essay is based on an asserted increase of juvenile crime, and it is demonstrated by the few preceding figures, that not only had it not increased, but that it had actually decreased 20 per cent. Mr. Worsley is even more seriously in error on other points. Having established a basis for his theory, he proceeds to show how and where the asserted increase has taken place,—that is, in the manufacturing districts. The second and third chapters of his book are principally occupied in developing and deploring the transition from the olden system of manufactures, the DOMESTIC, so called, to the FACTORY system; and he sums up his views and gives full vent to his excited feelings in the following burning terms:—" There is in truth presented to the inquirer, in the heart of the factory, an assemblage of the vile of human beings, a fermenting mass of sin and vice, such as we may well doubt was ever before concentrated in one burning focus. It seems as if the mighty capacities of steam had lent an impetus, not only to the industry and ingenuity of man, but an equal impetus to all his faculties and contrivances of vice. The interior of most of our factories is a school of iniquity, from which it is generally stated that few depart without learning something evil,—the comparatively ignorant become proficients in wickedness, the moral are made bad, and the bad depraved !"

It might suffice, in reply to this rhapsody of sentimentalism, to quote again the words of the Rev. J. Clay, Chaplain of Preston Gaol,—but those will not have been forgotten. Yet the same authority may be allowed to speak once more. On page 54 of his able and instructive Report for 1849, these words occur, immediately following an extended allusion to the efforts of mill-owners to enlighten and moralize those employed by them :—" We can now understand the reason of the small ratio of crime to population in Preston. No committal for *any offence*, no summons to the Town Hall, of Messrs. Horrocks and Miller's hands, numbering about 2000, or of Messrs. Catterals', numbering about 800, has taken place for two years. How strongly do these facts negative the *assumption* which imputes crime to the manufacturing *system! The cotton factory permits fewer opportunities for the growth and practice of dishonesty, and, in the hands of good and wise*

*masters, not only provides regular and remunerative labour,
but also promotes the mental and spiritual cultivation of
the labourers, with a regularity and success unattainable
where employment is less systematic, and where the work-
men are more scattered."*

But to stop here would be only to put one opinion
against another. Mr. Worsley's statistics relative to the
comparative juvenile criminality of the manufacturing and
agricultural counties must now be examined. He gives
them briefly enough, at page 107.

	Criminals, 1846.		Juvenile Criminals,1846.	
—	Total Number.	Proportion to Popula- tion, 1 in	Total Number.	Proportion to Popula- tion, 1 in
Agricultural Counties	10,119	768	2905	2678
Manufacturing Counties	14,988	542	4871	1668

The group of manufacturing counties comprises *Middlesex, Surrey, Worcestershire, Derbyshire, Gloucestershire,
Nottinghamshire,* Cheshire, Lancashire, Yorkshire, Staffordshire, Warwickshire, and Leicestershire. The agricultural
section includes the remaining twenty-eight counties, and
Wales.

It would be an utter waste of words, after what has been
said in the chapter on the " Comparative Morality of the
Agricultural and the Manufacturing Counties," to elaborate
again the reasons for excluding all the counties *in italics*
from the category of manufacturing counties; and also for
excluding Wales, Cumberland, Westmoreland, Northum-

berland, Durham, Cornwall, and Monmouth, from the
category of agricultural counties.   It is an axiom in
statistics, as in other sciences, to compare only things
which are *comparable*.   It is trifling, nay it is monstrously
absurd, to lump together forty counties and twelve
counties respectively—counties presenting such a variety
and complexity of social and industrial organization, under two great designations, each having a meaning and a
definiteness, with which one-third at least of the entire
fifty-two cannot be brought to square!   It is confidently
assumed, therefore, that the reasons for confining any
comparison of the manufacturing with the agricultural
counties, as to the respective ratios of crime, to six in the
former case, and twenty-two in the latter, cannot be im-
pugned.   Then, how will the case stand in 1845, which is
selected, because the populations for that year are already
calculated?

Juvenile Crime, 1844 to 1846,—average.

COUNTIES.	Number of Offences.	Ratio to all Offences.	Population.	Ratio to Pop. 1 in
6 Manufacturing - -	2191	30·1	5,163,195	2356
22 Agricultural - - -	2448	28	5,796,788	2367
* 3 Mining - - -	188	24	859,303	4570
† 5 Others - - - -	260	27·3	1,048,604	4040
Gloucester and Worcester	525	34·6	694,553	1322
Surrey - - - - -	319	33·7	629,306	1972
Middlesex - - - -	1549	35·6	1,677,536	1083
All England - - - -	7480	30·4	15,869,285	2121

Here, again, Mr. Worsley's *facts* (mistakes they should
* Cornwall, Durham, and Monmouth.
. † Cumberland, Derby, Northumberland, Notts, and Westmoreland.

be called) break down, and his whole theory goes with them. The elaborate elimination of the hated and evil mercantile and manufacturing influences, eloquent and able in other respects though it is, all goes for nothing, nay, is absolutely either purely imaginative, or sophistical. "The baseless fabric of a vision" never vanished more palpably to the waking sense, than does Mr. Worsley's whole system before these few figures. But the case may be further strengthened. Look at this Table:—

COUNTIES.	1842. Juvenile Crime.	1846. Crime, pro Ratio to 1842.	1846. Actual Crime.	1846. Decrease.
Cheshire - - -	288	308	229	26
Lancashire - -	1200	1310	864	34
Staffordshire - -	354	384	265	31
Warwick - - -	334	359	318	12
York - - - -	594	634	459	28

As it has already been proved, that the whole decrease of juvenile crime in all England, excluding Middlesex, betwixt 1842 and 1847, was 20 per cent., it follows from the preceding figures, that the decrease of juvenile crime in the manufacturing counties is much greater than in the agricultural; and it must be especially noted that the above ratios are not corrected for the different proportions of ages, &c., the data for such correction not existing. The correction would unquestionably diminish the ratio of juvenile crime in the manufacturing counties, and increase it in the agricultural. It is readily admitted, though it is an admission which, if advantage was taken of the total oversight of all such considerations by Mr. Worsley, need not be made, that 1846 was a year of great prosperity compared with 1842, and therefore, that it is not a fair criterion of the increase or decrease of juvenile crime. The admission, however, *is* made, but with this remark, that even if it should appear that juvenile crime in parallel years with 1842 showed an increase, Mr. Worsley's whole theory loses nothing of its inconclusiveness and absurdity, seeing it was built on data which, properly interpreted, directly disprove it.

It may be remarked in passing, that 1847, which was a year of considerable privation and suffering, and of greatly increased crime, as compared with 1844, 1845, and 1846, still shows an actual decrease of 9 per cent. in the number of juvenile offences as compared with 1842, even after adding all the convictions under the Juvenile Offenders Act, which came into operation in July in that year.

The year 1848 was nearly parallel to 1842 in the distress of the people, and in social disorganization and tumult. For that year the return of offences committed by juveniles is defective for those under fifteen years of age. The returns of former years, however, show that the proportion of offences committed by this section of the juvenile population is small, compared with the proportion committed by juveniles from fifteen to twenty years of age,—the one averaging about 6·0, and the other 24 centesimal parts. If, then, the proportions of crime committed by the latter class in 1848, did not exceed the same class of offences in 1842, it is proximally fair to infer, so neither did the former class. The following short Table will show how the fact stood, as respects the offences committed by persons fifteen to twenty years of age :—

—	1842. Actual Crime.	1848. Crime calculated for Increase of Population.	1848. Actual Crime.	Difference in Centesimal Parts.
Total Juvenile Crime	6762	7318	7066	3·4 less.
Total, deducting } Middlesex	5682	6152	5793	6·0 ,,

It is quite true that *all crime* in 1848, allowing for the increase of population, was less by 11 per cent. than in 1842; the actual crime being 29,427, the calculated, 33,104; but the fact remains, that juvenile crime was less in 1848 than in 1842. If the analysis be carried further, it gives these results for the five principal manufacturing counties :—

COUNTIES.	1842. Actual Crime.	1848. Calculated Crime.	1848. Actual Crime.	Difference in Centesimal Parts.
Chester - - -	229	251	246	2·0 less
Lancaster - -	944	1080	854	20·0 ,,
Stafford - - -	283	323	266	18·0 ,,
Warwick - - -	270	303	368	20·0 more
York - - - -	475	515	431	16·0 less
TOTAL - -	2201	2472	2165	12·4 less

The demonstration is again complete, that juvenile crime has not increased since 1842, but on the contrary, has decreased—the decrease being greatest in the manufacturing counties; as it is clear that, if in these the decrease is greater than on the average of all England, the remaining counties must fall below the average decrease of all England.

But why is the investigation of juvenile crime confined to the short cycle of 1842 to 1846? It will strike all persons accustomed to such inquiries, as somewhat singular that Mr. Worsley should have confined his comparison to the limited cycle of 5 years. Whether he did make any further investigation is at least doubtful. There seems strong internal evidence that the Table quoted from the Criminal Returns of 1847 was his *sole basis*. Be that as it may, in confining himself to that basis, he has committed another, and even more fatal error. He contends for a constantly and rapidly augmenting ratio of juvenile crime, and it is conclusively shown that, in place of augmentation, there was diminution. It will now be as conclusively shown that the diminution was not confined to the cycle from 1842 to 1846, but had been going on from 1836; so that Mr. Worsley has committed a double blunder: first, in mistaking the meaning of the Table before him; and second, in neglecting to examine the ratio of juvenile offences prior to 1842. The following Table will supply Mr. Worsley's omission,—observing that the years 1836 and 1845 represent the average of 1835 and 1837, and 1844 and 1846, respectively.

Juvenile Crime in 1836 *and* 1845.

—	Total Offences.		Ratio to Pop.		Ratio to all Crime.	
	1836.	1845.	1836.	1845.	1836.	1845.
			One in	One in		
6 Manufacturing Counties	2214	2191	1981	2356	35·5	30·1
22 Agricultural ditto -	2680	2448	1992	2367	33·	28·0
3 Mining ditto -	151	188	4809	4570	28·	24·
*5 other Counties - -	266	260	3603	4040	32·	27·3
Gloucester and Worcester	420	525	1504	1322	35·	34·6
Middlesex - - - -	1250	1549	1174	1083	37·3	35.6
Surrey - - - - -	378	319	1414	1972	38·5	33·7
All England - - - -	7359	7480	1908	2121	34·4	30·4

Here is most striking proof, comparing two cycles of
three years together (each cycle embracing a period of
prosperity), that the proportion of juvenile *to all crime,* has
declined in the whole of England, and in all sections or
groups of counties; and that the proportion of juvenile crime
to the population had greatly fallen in the latter cycle, in 34
out of 40 *counties,* the exceptions being the mining counties,
and the counties of Gloucester, Worcester, and Middlesex;
and even in these, the increase of juvenile crime is not nearly
so conspicuous as is its decrease in the other counties. It is
surely a most legitimate conclusion from the last Table,
that the decrease in juvenile crime is not accidental, but
indicates the constant and steady action of some ameliorating process acting upon the rising generation; for it
must be especially noted, that the ratio of the total crime
of each section was nearly alike for all England, and for
the manufacturing and agricultural sections of the counties
at the two periods; and therefore, as the proportion of

* Cumberland, Northumberland, Notts, Derby, and Westmoreland.

juvenile offences was less in 1845 than in 1836, the proportion of *adult* crime must have been greater. The decrease in the one class simultaneously with an increase in the other, indicates the specific action of some moral influence on the juvenile population ; and whatever that influence may be, the fact that, after all the deteriorating and demoralizing process of suffering betwixt 1839 and 1843, juvenile crime in 1845 was less by 13 per cent. than in 1836, implies that the influence is one of great power, and is as permanent as it is powerful.

It must not be implied, from the course of these observations, that the great proportion of juvenile crime is not a serious matter, or deserving of patient investigation as to its forms, sources, and tendencies. All that is intended to show is, that THE* authority on this question is completely worthless ; and to direct inquiry according to correct principles of analysis and induction. To mistake the diagnosis of a complaint, is to aggravate the disease, if not to kill the patient. It may be repeated, and with increased emphasis, that it is not the manufacturing system, and especially the factory system, that increases juvenile crime. Lancashire, and the West Riding of York, represent that system, and both show a diminishing ratio of juvenile offences ; and let it be especially noted that, if all the crime of Yorkshire were thrown upon the West Riding, it would still rank with the county of Lincoln, which is at the head of the agricultural counties. No benefit, but, on the contrary,

---

* Mr. Worsley's book is quoted as THE authority, because it has become a text-book. In point of accuracy of statement, patience of research, and general breadth and correctness of view, it is far behind Mr. Beggs's volume, which is a valuable contribution to our information relative to the criminal classes.

positive mischief only, can arise from speculations as to
CAUSES, until the PHENOMENA under consideration are ex-
haustively analysed. ↱ It is painful to see a vast amount
of talent and labour expended in bringing together the
incidental notices of social conditions and social evils,
which by their very isolation acquire an apparent magnitude and importance which they would instantly lose, if
relieved by the filling up of the entire picture of society.
Any person accustomed to refer to the authorities quoted
by public writers on the subject of crime, cannot but be
aware what a thoroughly one-sided view of things is presented, partly because one set of phenomena only is selected, and partly because what is selected is made to
clench a foregone conclusion, or becomes the ridiculously
narrow basis of an entire theory. Mr. Worsley's book is
again reluctantly referred to in proof of this.

At page 98, he quotes the Reports on " Trades and
Manufactures " for 1843, as follows, prefacing the quotation thus:—" The following extracts will convey some idea
of the destitution of the manufacturing districts in regard
to education :—the sub-commissioner states, that three-
fourths of the children examined by him, even in those
places in which the *means of instruction are the most abundant, could neither read nor write ; that the ignorance of
the young people throughout the district is absolute;* that
this is proved by the testimony of ministers of religion of
all denominations, and by that of the employers and their
agents of all classes; and that the main causes of this
neglect of education are here, as everywhere else, the early
age at which children are taken from school to work,—
their inability to attend evening schools after the labour of
the day,—and the utter inefficiency of Sunday-schools to

compensate for the loss of day-schooling; numerous instances occurring of children who had been for years in
regular attendance at these schools, who, on examination,
were found incapable of distinguishing one letter from
another." Now, ninety-nine persons in one hundred would
understand by the designation, "manufacturing districts,"
the great seats of the cotton and woollen manufactures ;
but on reference to the Report itself, it is found that the
sub-commissioner is speaking of the Staffordshire Potteries
only, containing a population of some 100,000 persons.
But the facts stated in the quotation exist nowhere, except in the brain of the sub-commissioner ; it is not justified by the evidence which is printed at length in the
Appendix, 1843. That evidence occupies upwards of 100
pages. On a careful analysis of the answers of children
under thirteen years of age, examined by the sub-commissioner, it is found that fifty-seven could read, twenty-one
could not read, and forty-three could not read, *but go to
Sunday-school*—in other words, they *cannot read as yet,
they are* LEARNING. So much for the evidence of the
children themselves.

The testimony of the overlookers is equally against the
sub-commissioner. Twenty-three of them stated that the
greater part of the children employed in the Potteries *can
read and write ;* eight stated that *all read and write ;* and
six that FEW READ AND WRITE. The fact is, that, as a
picture of the state of education in the Potteries, the statement is absolutely untrue ; and it is advisedly so said. The
manner, too, in which the quotation is introduced in Mr.
Worsley's book can only lead to error, and indeed has done
so ; and is a specimen of loose statement and writing,
which in so accomplished a scholar is not a little marvel-

I 2

lous. Statements *such* as these, *so* prefaced, pass current
as succinct embodiments of *great facts;* just as the iterated
statement (falsehood ?), " that one half of the children of
Great Britain can neither read nor write," has become the
cuckoo note of men whose position demands of them that
they should verify every statement involving facts of so
momentous an import, before they place upon them the
stamp of their authority.

Further observations on the subject of juvenile crime are
unnecessary after what has been said in the chapter on the
Criminal Class, and it must be dismissed with this em·
phatic assertion, that there is no evidence, as yet, which
shows that the youth of the indigent and really operative
population are retrograding, *but the contrary ;* and that all
the evidence on the subject of juvenile crime goes to show,
what all other evidence on the subject shows, that the
mass of crime is committed by a criminal class, whose
real history is yet to be written.

RATIO OF CRIME COMMITTED BY PERSONS BETWIXT TWENTY AND THIRTY YEARS OF AGE.

THE special notice bestowed by public writers on juvenile crime has originated in a common belief that it was *specifically* the increasing class of crime. Magistrates, statisticians, and journalists have all enlarged upon it, as THE most alarming fact in connexion with the whole subject of crime. How completely they have been in error is now made plain. But it will startle them and certain essayists, to be told that, whilst juvenile crime has been decreasing, and the total of crime either greatly retarded in its onward progress, or actually diminishing, the amount of crime committed by persons betwixt 20 and 30 years has augmented in a degree perfectly astounding; and the more so, because of the facts just stated. As the fruit of the investigation of the ratios of crime at four sections of ages, for the purposes stated in Chapter III., the following figures are now given :—

Ratio of Crime to each 100,000 *of the Population at the undermentioned Ages, in the undermentioned Groups of Counties, and for all England.*

	1836. Average of 1835, 1836, & 1837.				
	Crime, under 20 Yrs.	Crime, 20 to 25 Years.	Crime, 25 to 30 Years.	Crime, 30 and upwds.	Total Crime.
6 Manufacturing Counties	108	257	274	130	143
22 Agricultural ditto -	108	331	328	129	152
3 Mining ditto -	43	160	157	72	74
Middlesex - - - -	213	368	331	189	231
Surrey - - - - -	176	296	295	140	183
Gloucester and Worcester	146	357	359	164	189
* 5 other Counties - -	59	173	172	88	87
All England - - -	114	289	292	132	152

1845.—*Average of* 1844, 1845, *and* 1846.

	Crime, under 20 Years.	Crime, 20 to 25 Years.	Crime, 25 to 30 Years.	Crime, 30 and upwds.	Total Crime.
6 Manufacturing Counties	89	331	258	128	140
22 Agricultural ditto	91	411	311	130	152
3 Mining ditto	45	238	185	90	90
Middlesex - - - -	230	529	344	194	261
Surrey - - - - -	126	392	221	111	150
Gloucester and Worcester	166	537	357	217	220
* 5 other Counties - -	53	229	181	65	90
All England - - -	103	381	280	132	156

The following Table shows the percentage of increase and decrease of the criminality in each group of counties, and for *all England*, at each section of ages :—

* Cumberland, Westmoreland, Northumberland, Derby, and Notts.

	20 Years and under. Inc. De.		20 to 25 Years. Inc. De.		25 to 30 Years. Inc. De.		30 and upwards. Inc. De.		Total Inc De.	
6 Manufacturing Counties	...	18	30	...	...	6	...	1	...	2
22 Agricultural ditto -	...	16	24	...	...	5	½	...	Par.	...
3 Mining ditto -	4	...	50	...	18	...	24	...	20	...
Middlesex ditto -	7½	...	44	...	4	...	2½	...	13	...
Surrey - - - - - -	...	29	32	...	...	25	...	20	...	17
Gloucester and Worcester -	14	...	51	...	Par.	...	33	...	16	...
5 other Counties - - - -	...	12	33	...	6	...	...	25	4	...
All England - - - - -	...	10	33	...	...	4	...	Par.	2½	...

It is quite true that the criminal returns, for the years compared, are constructed on a different classification of ages. In 1835, 1836, and 1837, the ages were divided into three sections, up to 21 years, and the criminals from 21 to 30 years of age formed a fourth section. In 1844, 1845, and 1846 the total of criminals *under* 30 were ranged in four sections, namely, under 15, aged 15 and under 20, aged 20 and under 25, aged 25 and *under* 30. In the latter cycle of years the total of criminals, comprised in the four sections, would comprise a smaller number than the total of the three sections in the former cycle. It is impossible accurately to adjust the relative numbers of criminals at each age in the respective periods ; but no error in the adjustment attempted can possibly destroy the GREAT FACT of an enormous increase of crime amongst the population from 20 to 30 years of age. If all the crime up to 21 years of age in the cycle of 1835, 1836, and 1837 were put against the crime committed up to 20 years of age, in 1844 to 1846 ; and all the crime committed betwixt 21 and 30 years of age, in the former cycle, against the crime committed betwixt 20 and 30 years in the latter cycle, juvenile crime would show a less *decrease,* and crime from 20 to 30 a smaller *increase* than is shown by the Table given ; but the stubborn fact would remain, that crime committed by persons betwixt 20 and 30 years of age was greatly augmented in the latter period.

If this be so, then public writers have been pursuing an *ignis-fatuus* in the investigation of the increase of crime, whilst looking for the sole, or principal, source of that increase (real or supposed) in juvenile offences. It is palpable that all the increase has been in the ages from 20 to 30, and that so great, as to neutralize an actual diminution of crime at the juvenile and the riper adult ages.

The fact is important, and it suggests the necessity of a careful and most exact analysis of the crime committed by the population betwixt 20 and 30, or say 15 and 30, with an especial reference to the determination of its peculiar character of turpitude or otherwise, its connexion with new organizations of society, or with alterations in the law, and the precise social position and moral status of the actual criminals. The inquiry, in fact, ought to comprise *all crime*. Voluminous as are the present returns, as to criminal offences, they are greatly deficient in the one important matter of moral data. The tests of the ability to read and write are of small value as moral indices. What is wanted is a clue to the conditions and circumstances which accompany crime, of whatever kind. The reading and writing test supplies one element —often a most deceptive one—where other, and even more potent elements, have been at work. The test is utterly valueless, indeed, on the assumption, *and it is only an assumption*, that it is a measure of other things—social status—home influences—intellectual tastes, and moral principle.

If the causes and sources of crime are to be known, the criminal must be tracked *home* to his *birth-place*, so to speak, so that his moral history may be revealed, and the exact incidence of the *cause or causes*, which have led to his divergence from the path of rectitude, may be measured. It is believed this is possible. Five years of careful inquiry and accurate registration would supply a world of facts bearing upon this precise point, of immeasurably greater value than fifty years of the speculations about marriage marks, and contrivances about prison discipline. The inquiry, to be worth anything, should embrace the following particulars :—

1. The birth-place of the criminal.
2. The parentage, occupation, and mode of life of parents.
3. His early education—what ?
4. His first employment, and its continuance.
5. Occupation at the time of his committal.
6. Whether convicted before, and how often.
7. For what offences.
8. When last employed, and where.

It is not expected that a criminal would, at all times, readily and honestly answer all these queries, but it would be possible, in the majority of instances, to eke out his communications by inquiry. The value of such materials would be incalculable. It might turn out that particular occupations offer special inducement to crime, and thus the counteractives might be suggested ; or it might prove that certain conditions of society give special opportunities to the commission of crime, and by a process of corruption, sap, undermine, and weaken the moral principle. But be that so or not, it does not admit of a moment's doubt

that five years of accurate records on all the points indicated, and a scientific classification of the same, would
solve more than one vexed question ; and, *perhaps,* suggest
some great social remedies.   Enough, and more than
enough, is done in some departments of administration, in
the minute record of facts.   It cannot be pleaded, that a
more elaborate registration of the FACTS of crime is either
too onerous, or would be more expensive, than the results
obtained would amply compensate.

ON THE VALUE OF THE TESTS APPLIED TO DETERMINE THE INFLUENCE OF IGNORANCE ON CRIME.

THE Government returns of crime contain, as is well known, Tables showing the degree of instruction of all offenders tried at the sessions and assizes. The latest returns, namely for the ten years ending in 1848, show that the proportion of those " unable to read and write," to all offenders, has gradually fallen, with several fluctuations, however, from 33·53 centesimal parts in 1839, to 31·93 parts in 1848. In 1844, the proportion was only 29·77. The greater proportion in 1848 is to be accounted for, most probably, by the distress of that year, causing a larger proportionate number of the very lowest and most ignorant of the population to commit crime, and more especially breaches of the peace. The proportion of offenders " able to read and write imperfectly " was 53·48 in 1839, 59·28 in 1844, and 56·38 in 1848. The proportion of those " able to read and write well " was 10·07, 8·12, and 9·83, for the same years respectively. The proportion of those who had received instruction superior to reading and writing well, was 0·32 in 1839, and 0·27 in 1848.

These figures demonstrate that instruction is on the increase amongst that portion of the population who commit crime, and afford a strong presumption that instruction,—

understanding by that term the ability to read and write,—
was gradually becoming more diffused throughout the population, at the period when the respective criminals were of
the age to receive it.   As upwards of 65 per cent. of all
crime is, on the average, committed by persons from fifteen
to thirty years of age, the diminution of the number " unable to read and write," and the increase of those " able to
read and write imperfectly," show the progress of instruction from 1823 to 1838, *and not its present state,* supposing school instruction to commence at the age of five years.
No doubt these indications of the progress of instruction
during that period, are affected by the degree of instruction
which the remaining proportion of criminals, say 35 per
cent., whose ages were thirty years and upwards, had received some time or other betwixt 1800 and 1823.   If, as
all the information attainable on the subject shows, the
progress of instruction was greatly accelerated after 1818,
then, it is fair to infer that the diminution in the number
of those " unable to read and write," and the increase of
those " able to read and write imperfectly," betwixt 1839
and 1848, represents the average progress of instruction
betwixt 1801 and 1839 ; and it is equally fair to infer that,
if the numbers of each class were given for the gradations of
age, rather than for the total of criminals, the indications,
such as they are, which the returns of the degree of instruction of criminals afford of the progress of instruction
amongst the population at large, would be more favourable
on the side of progress.

It may, however, be seriously doubted whether an inter-
pretation has not been put on these figures which they do
not warrant ; namely, that they show the influence which
instruction has upon crime.   Laborious Tables have been

compiled, and lengthy treatises written, founded upon these data and the marriage marks combined, to show that crime is affected by them—in other words, that where the marriage marks, and the proportion of criminals " unable to read and write," preponderate, there crime is greatest, relatively to the population. Enough has been said in previous chapters, on the irrelevancy of these facts, without the comparative number of the operative classes to all others being first ascertained ; because, the great bulk of offences being committed by persons of that class, and the criminal class, *per se*, it is obviously necessary to determine the relative proportion of these two sections of the population to the middle and upper classes, before any correct inference can be drawn from the proportion of those " unable to read and write." It may be that a higher proportion of such criminals in a particular county, *to all criminals,* indicates a higher, rather than a lower degree of instruction, when the relative proportion of all classes of the population is ascertained.

The opinions combated admit of a simple test. If elementary instruction in reading and writing is of the value stated, or may be taken as an index of other and more powerful influences, then, if the proportion of the criminals who can read is increasing, there ought to be a diminution in crime. The following Tables will show whether that is so, or not :—

Instruction of Criminals, 1836.

—	Ratio of Crime to Population.	Number of Criminals who cannot read or write.	Proportion to Population.	Proportion to all Crime.	Numb. of Criminals who can read and write imperfectly.	Proportion to Population.	Proportion to all Crime.
6 Manufacturing Counties	695	2305	1902	36·5	3033	1446	53·
22 Agricultural Counties	655	2979	1792	36·5	3905	1367	48·7
Middlesex	437	976	1503	29·	1926	761	58·
All England	657	7385	1883	34·5	10783	1302	52·5

Instruction of Criminals, 1845.

—	Ratio of Crime to Population.	Total Number cannot read or write.	Proportion to Population.	Proportion to all Crime.	Numb. read and write imperfectly.	Proportion to Population.	Proportion to all Crime.
6 Manufacturing Counties	710	2339	2207	32·2	4274	1208	59·
22 Agricultural Counties	659	2885	2044	32·3	5161	1123	59·
Middlesex	383	1113	1507	25·5	2521	665	58·
All England	641	7437	2133	30·2	14593	1080	59·

It will be seen, at a glance, that whilst the ratio of all crime in the period was nearly at par, except in the county of Middlesex, the proportion of those "who could not read and write" had fallen 4·3 ; and the proportion of those who could "read and write imperfectly" had risen 6·5 on the average of all England. Now, according to the theory under consideration, crime ought to have diminished, but it was at par ; and there is the further contradiction of the theory, that the total of the offences committed by both sections had risen 2·2 per cent. The theory is palpably at fault. But does it follow that because crime has not fallen, the more general diffusion of instruction has failed to do any good ? That may be seriously doubted. If there be any truth in what has been advanced respecting the influence of town populations, it may be reasonably conjectured that the criminal class, specifically so called, has increased during the cycle of nine years; and if so, it is obvious that crime has continued stationary, because all other classes of the community have committed less crime. The conditions leading to crime have been aggravated to an extent which has counteracted the repressive influence of the increased instruction given. This view is strengthened by the fact that in Middlesex, which during the whole fifty years of the century has shown the highest ratio of crime, and which notoriously harbours the greatest relative number of the criminal class, crime had increased betwixt 1836 and 1845. There it would seem that the action of the conditions which always accompany a high ratio of crime, namely, great density and aggregation of the population, and great wealth and luxury, had more than counterbalanced the increased instruction of the people; for in that county the proportion of criminals who could " read and write imperfectly " had considerably increased. Be this as it may, the facts patent on the Table demonstrate the futility of the test on which so much reliance is placed.

But the futility of that test may be more strikingly shown by a comparison of the counties of Kent and Lancaster, as follows :—

—	Ratio of Crime, 1845.	Ratio of Criminals who cannot read and write to all Criminals.	Ratio of same to Population, 1 in	Ratio of Criminals who read and write imperfectly to all Criminals.	Ratio of same to Pop., 1 in
Kent - -	632	33·0	2062	59·0	1159
Lancaster	686	46·7	1333	46·8	1334

Similar instances might readily be given.

Now, this one case puts the theory in question entirely at fault. Lancaster, according to the theory, ought to have considerably more crime than Kent, but it has less. Ignorance, as tested by the ability to "read and write," is vastly preponderant;—it has 13·7 per cent. more criminals who "can neither read nor write," and 12·8 per cent. less who "can read and write imperfectly." Kent shows, therefore, a far higher degree of instruction, but its criminality is in the proportion of 158 criminals in 100,000 of its population, to 146 in 100,000 in the population of Lancashire, or about 7½ per cent. excess in Kent.

This instance, and the Table preceding, seem incontestably to prove that the instruction test is of little value, taken *alone*. Apart from these proofs, there are most obvious independent grounds for such a conclusion. The elementary instruction of reading and writing, even accompanied by a course of moral training such as is generally found in the schools frequented by the children of the middle classes, is only one of the many influences which form the mental and moral character of a people. It is a vulgar error to speak of school instruction, as though it comprised all that constitutes education in its proper sense. Men are acted upon, at all ages, from childhood upwards, by a vast number of circumstances, distinct from school instruction, and to a large extent, independent of its presence or absence. It is almost superfluous to name the examples of the household, and of the sphere in which a child moves, and the action of religious teaching through its public ordinances. Again, the final influence of scholastic instruction is very largely affected by the after associations and circumstances of the man. When he has quitted the school, it needs no laboured argument to show that the same amount of elementary training may be turned to far higher advantage where the after appliances of mental and moral improvement are most abundant. Now, will any sane man maintain that the rustic scholar, who has got a fair amount of scholastic knowledge, is on the same level of advantages, as to his subsequent progress in intelligence, with the artizan's child of equal scholastic attainments, but surrounded by a hundred means of instruction, of which the rustic knows nothing?—some, indeed, dependent on his willingness to embrace them, but not a few which will act upon him, whether he be passive or active. Place the two together at 21 years of age, and note the difference in general intelligence, sagacity, and knowledge of men and things, and strike the balance! True, whilst in the large towns there are so many means of acquiring knowledge—the press, the pulpit, the public meetings, the mechanics' institute—contact with the more educated classes, and the constant intellectual encounter with his fellows, often clever and superior men,—there are also many corrupting influences. Yet it may be gravely doubted whether the coarseness—

almost amounting to brutality,—which is displayed by a considerable section of the agricultural labourers, the sources
of which have been so graphically described of late by
various writers, does not indicate the presence of more
deteriorating moral influences in the rural districts, than
accompany the seductions and temptations of the towns,
so far as these seductions and temptations act upon the
indigenous or actual working population. The county of
Lancaster is a case in point. It is quite inexplicable,
looking to the figures given above, and coupling them with
the well-known influence of Irish immigration, and the
presence of a large criminal class, how the total ratio of
crime there is less than in Kent; except on the one supposition, that the *industrious* classes (in the main an indigenous class) are above the average morality of the kingdom. If this be the solution, then is Mr. Clay's opinion
established, that the factory system admits of a "far higher
and better application of the means of intellectual and
moral culture than any other organization of labour,"—an
opinion which, in spite of preconceived notions and strong
prejudices to the contrary, is fixing itself in the general
belief.

It must not be concluded from what precedes, that the
efficiency of public instruction is denied, always supposing that such instruction includes what all instruction
which aims at moral results *must include*,—the training of
the whole being, physically, intellectually, and *morally*.
All that is objected against, is the fallaciousness of the
"capacity to read and write," as a test of the presence of
moral influences and results. The same degree of attainment in these mere elements of knowledge, or more properly, these mental instruments for the attainment of

knowledge, may be associated with the widest divergences in the degrees of moral culture ; and no greater or more fatal mistake can be made, than to rest satisfied with mental cultivation alone, no matter what its form, as the security for the right moral conduct of man in the domestic, social, and spiritual relations of life.   A nation, relying upon the intellectual refinement and polish of *all* its members, even for permanence and safety, rests upon a quicksand.   There is neither in individuals, nor in nations, any solid basis of greatness or permanence apart from the pervading and controlling force of moral principle—and moral principle, in its proper and specific sense, is only another name for Religion.

BOOKS PUBLISHED

BY

CHARLES GILPIN,

5, BISHOPSGATE STREET WITHOUT,

LONDON.

Agent for Scotland:

ADAM & CHARLES BLACK, Edinburgh.

Agent for Ireland:

J. B. GILPIN, Dublin.

REED and PARDON, Printers, Paternoster Row.

The Age and its Architects : Ten Chapters on the People and the Times. By EDWIN PAXTON HOOD. Fcap. 8vo., price 5s.

The figures of the Statist will generally, in the course of the work, be conveyed by Portraits and descriptions of the people with whom we live, and the places in which we live. It will be a lucid analysis of the age and its virtues, vices, and views. Historical, Æsthetic, and Didactic Delineations of the Development of Individual, Domestic, and Social Regeneration. Written especially for the youthful aspirant to a life of intelligent labour and usefulness. The nature of the work may be gathered from the list of the topics of the various chapters.

CHAPTER I.—THE BATTLES AND CONQUESTS OF INDUSTRY.
„ II.—THE VICTORIAN COMMONWEALTH.
„ III.—THE PHYSIQUE OF A GREAT CITY.
„ IV.—THE ARCADIAS OF ENGLAND.
„ V.—THE WRONGS OF THE PEOPLE.
„ VI.—THE SINS OF THE PEOPLE.
„ VII.—THE MISSION OF THE SCHOOLMASTER.
„ VIII.—WOMAN THE REFORMER.
„ IX.—WESTWARD HO!
„ X.—MODERN UTOPIAS.

The Pastor's Wife. A Memoir of Mrs. Sherman, of Surrey Chapel. By her HUSBAND. With a Portrait, Eighth Thousand, foolscap 8vo., price 5s.

"This constitutes one of the most tender, beautiful, instructive, and edifying narratives that for a long time has come under our notice. * * * We anticipate for it a very extended popularity and usefulness among the mothers and daughters of England."—*Christian Witness*, January, 1849.

"This volume deserves a large circulation, and we feel it a pleasure to commend its perusal to the various classes of our readers, especially to those whose sex may enable them to tread in Mrs. Sherman's steps."—*Nonconformist*, January 24, 1849.

GENERAL KLAPKA'S NEW WORK ON THE HUNGARIAN WAR.

Memoirs of the War of Independence in Hungary.
By General Klapka, late Secretary at War to the Hungarian Commonwealth ; and Commandant of the Fortrefs of Komorn. 2 vols., poft 8vo., price 21s.

This work will be found one of deep intereft to all, as containing an authentic hiftorical record of the Hungarian War from the pen of a General Officer engaged in it; and efpecially to thofe who have fympathized with the ftruggles and facrifices of the Hungarian Nation in defence of its rights and its liberties. The author, officially connected with the Council of War, enjoying the confidence and friendfhip of the illuftrious Koffuth, and faithful to the laft to the interefts of his fuffering country, is well qualified to give fuch information as will place in a clear light the true character of that ftruggle which has recently defolated one of the faireft countries of Europe, and facrificed in the field or by the executioner many of the nobleft of her fons. General Klapka, having been perfonally acquainted with the principal Officers who were fhot or hanged at Arad, Pefth, &c., by command of the Auftrians, propofes to give in the courfe of the work fhort biographical fketches with a narrative of the circumftances attending the deaths of thofe Officers. The publication of this work is undertaken with the defire to affift fome of the Hungarian Refugees now in this country.

The Water Cure. Letters from Grafenberg in the years 1843-4-5, and 6. By John Gibbs. 12mo., cloth, price 4s. 6d.

"The inquirers after health, the philanthropift, and the medical practitioner will do well to read Mr. Gibbs' book, for which we thank him, and which we beg very fincerely to recommend to careful perufal."—*Nonconformift*, September 18, 1849.

"We ftrongly recommend its perufal."—*Limerick Chronicle.*

8vo., cloth, price 12s.

SAND AND CANVASS:

A Narrative of Adventures in Egypt, with a sojourn among the Artists in Rome, &c. With illustrations.

By SAMUEL BEVAN.

" The random high spirits of this book give *salt* to the sand, and *colour* to the canvass."—*Athenæum.*

" The truth is never disguised, but things are mentioned with an air of sincerity that is irresistible. We never recollect to have opened a book which possessed this charm in anything approaching to the same degree. It captivates and excites, giving reality and interest to every incident that is introduced."—*Morning Post.*

8vo., price 7s.

THE DEMERARA MARTYR.

MEMOIRS OF THE REV. JOHN SMITH,
Missionary to Demerara.

By Edwin Angel Wallbridge. With a Preface by the Rev. W. G. Barrett.

" There will one day be a resurrection of names and reputations, as certainly as of bodies."—*John Milton.*

" The book is a worthy monument to the distinguished Martyr whose history forms its leading subject. * * * A valuable contribution to the cause of freedom, humanity, and justice in Demerara."—*Patriot.*

" We have perused this work with mixed feelings of pain and admiration; pain, arising from the sense of wrong and misery inflicted on a good man; admiration, that the author has so fully redeemed his friend and brother minister from calumnies and misrepresentations of Satanic malice and wickedness."—*Standard of Freedom*, August 30, 1848.

8vo., cloth, price 6s. 6d.

A POPULAR LIFE OF GEORGE FOX,
The First of the Quakers.

By JOSIAH MARSH.

Compiled from his Journal and other authentic sources, and interspersed with remarks on the imperfect reformation of the Anglican Church, and the consequent spread of dissent.

The work abounds with remarkable incidents, which pourtray a vivid picture of the excited feelings that predominated during those eventful periods of our history—the Commonwealth and the Restoration.

12mo., cloth, price 3s. 6d.

THE ISLAND OF CUBA.

Its Resources, Progress, and Prospects, considered especially in relation to the influence of its prosperity on the interests of the British West India Colonies.

By R. R. MADDEN, M.R.I.A.

"This little volume contains a large amount of valuable information, intimately connected with the progress of society and happiness of man."—*Christian Times.*

"We recommend the book to the perusal of all who are interested in the great work of negro emancipation."—*Standard of Freedom.*

"As supplying the latest information concerning Cuba, Mr. Madden's book is extremely valuable."—*Economist.*

"We cordially recommend the volume."—*Anti-Slavery Reporter.*

Fcap. 8vo., cloth, gilt edges, price 3s. 6d.

CAPTAIN SWORD AND CAPTAIN PEN.

A Poem. By LEIGH HUNT.

The third Edition, with a new Preface, remarks on War, and Notes detailing the horrors on which the Poem is founded.

> "Probably in no work of one hundred pages was there ever amassed so much of horror. * * * We admire its brilliancy, and are amazed at its force."—*Morning Chronicle.*

> "Mr. Leigh Hunt's Poem and Notes, together with the excellent Prefaces, are eminently calculated to diffuse a more rational and Christian spirit among all classes of readers. We recommend them to every father of a family and guardian of youth."—*Morning Advertiser.*

18mo., cloth, price 2s.

WHITTIER'S POEMS

The Poetical Works of John G. Whittier. Reprinted from the Boston 8vo. edition, containing Appendix and copious Notes.

12mo., cloth, price 4s.

THE PEASANTRY OF ENGLAND.

An Appeal on behalf of the Working Classes; in which the causes which have led to their present impoverished and degraded condition, and the means by which it may best be permanently improved, are clearly pointed out.

By G. M. PERRY.

Poft 8vo., price 7s.

THE AUTOBIOGRAPHY OF A
WORKING MAN.

By "ONE WHO HAS WHIṢTLED AT THE PLOUGH."

This work contains the "Barrack Life of a Dragoon;" what the author did to fave Britain from a Revolution; his Court Martial and Punifhment at Birmingham; the confpiracy of the Secret Committee of the Trade Unions in London to "Affaffinate the Cabinet Minifters, and Capture the Palace, Royal Family, and Bank of England;" how planned and how prevented.

"Here is a genuine, frefh, and thoroughly true book; fomething really worth reading and remembering."— *Manchefter Examiner.*

"The well known author of this work, who has attracted much public attention, and has acquired a well merited reputation, has done the public a great fervice by publifhing his autobiography."—*Economift.*

"This is one of the moft interefting works which has come under our notice for a long time. It is the genuine record of the inner and outer life of a genuine working man. * * * There are few writings in our language, which, for power of graphic defcription, furpafs the letters by him under the fignature of 'One who has Whiftled at the Plough;' and in his autobiography we find the fame facility of defcription, &c."—*Leeds Times.*

Fourth edition, 32mo., cloth, price 1s.

UNITED STATES OF AMERICA
By ARCHIBALD PRENTICE.

A Tour in the United States, with two Lectures on Emigration, delivered in the Mechanics' Inftitution, Manchefter.

Charles Gilpin's Readings for Railways. Edited by Popular Authors.

The Publisher has, in common with a large proportion of those whose engagements necessitate considerable travel by railway, much regretted that the class of literature generally to be met with at the various stations, so far from being calculated to improve and to instruct, is mostly composed of Novels and Romances of at least very questionable tendency. Some of these, taken from the French school of novelists, are such as no prudent or careful parent would permit to be placed in the hands of a son or daughter. The Publisher believes that it is perfectly possible to secure a class of reading, which, while not inferior in interest to those books which now almost monopolize the station tables, shall yet possess a decidedly moral tone and instructive tendency; and seeing the amount of time spent in travelling, an amount which it is probable will yet greatly increase, he has determined to make the attempt to introduce such literature for railways as may be approved by the great mass of the reading public. To carry out these views, he has made arrangements with able and popular writers, and has already published volume the first of the series, edited by Leigh Hunt.

The volumes, price One Shilling each, will be published in a neat form, and in clear readable type, and may be obtained at the various Railway Stations in the United Kingdom.

Readings for Railways; or, Anecdotes and other Short Stories, Reflections, Maxims, Characteristics, Passages of Wit, Humour, and Poetry, &c.; together with Points of Information on Matters of General Interest, collected in the course of his own reading. By Leigh Hunt. Royal 18mo., price 1s.

"Leigh Hunt's name would beautify any production, even trivial in itself, with the glory of his early fame. The book will prove a valuable antidote to railway weariness to whomsoever will take it in hand, as his railway companion."—*Morning Chronicle.*

₊ The second volume is now ready. Edited by J. B. Syme.

Juvenile Depravity. The Prize Essay on Juvenile Depravity. By the Rev. H. WORSLEY, A.M., Easton Rectory, Suffolk. To this Essay on Juvenile Depravity, as connected with the causes and practices of Intemperance, and the effectual barrier opposed by them to education, the above Prize of 100*l.* was awarded by the Adjudicators, Dr. Harris of Cheshunt; the Rev. James Sherman, Surrey Chapel; and Dr. Vaughan of Harrow. Post 8vo., price 5s.

"We earnestly commend this very able Essay to the early attention of those whose philanthropy leads them to seek a remedy for the fearful amount of juvenile depravity which now gangrenes society, and will prove fatal if not checked and removed. The author admirably uses his statistics, and shows an intimate knowledge of human nature, in its multifarious circumstances."—*Christian Examiner*, April, 1849.

"It is impossible to read many sentences of this volume without perceiving that you are in the company of a Christian philanthropist—a man who is bent, as far as in him lies, on the removal of a great national evil; and who has sufficient patience and courage to investigate the sources of that evil, to examine with candour the various remedies proposed for its removal, and to point out with honesty that which he believes to be the only appropriate and effectual remedy."—*Teetotal Times*, April, 1849.

"Mr. Worsley's is unquestionably a very able treatise." —*Patriot*, April, 1849.

The Rhyming Game; a Historiette. 16mo., sewed, price 6d.

This little book is designed as a winter evening recreation for young persons. Its object is, that of calling up their ideas into ready exercise, and habituating the mind to a prompt and accurate description of objects, as well as a more subtle delineation of thoughts and feelings; and it has particularly in view the monition that, even in their recreations, they may remember "l'utile," as well as "l'agréable."

Juvenile Depravity. An Inquiry into the Extent
and Causes of Juvenile Depravity. Dedicated, by special
permission, to the Right Hon. the Earl of Carlisle. By
THOMAS BEGGS, late Secretary of the Health of Towns'
Association, and author of " Lectures on the Moral Elevation of the People." 8vo., price 5s.

"Few men were better qualified to deal with such a
case than Mr. Beggs, whose lot it has been largely to be
mixed up with the working classes, and who has made
their characters, habits, and circumstances, the subject of
his special study. He is, moreover, a man of strong
penetrating intellect, and possesses in a high degree whatever is needful to constitute a student of human nature.
Let all read Mr. Begg's volume. A heart brought very
largely into sympathy with the subject could scarcely
read a chapter of it without tears. Its revelations are
those of the darkest chambers of spiritual death and
moral desolation. The work has our cordial commen-
dation. It is one of the class of books which cannot
be too widely circulated."—*British Banner*, August 25,
1849.

"Mr. Beggs writes with all the confidence which a
practical knowledge of the subject has given him, and it
is impossible to peruse the pages of his work without ob-
taining a fearful insight into the extent of the moral
depravity of the lower orders of society. In the paths
of vice in which his reverend competitor fears to tread,
there Mr. Beggs boldly steps forward, and denounces
while he exposes those gigantic and appalling evils, which
must be brought to light before they can be effectually
grappled with and overcome."—*Journal of Public
Health*, July, 1849.

"Whether we regard the graphic picture of the
actual condition of the neglected classes, or the important collection of original and selected statistics which
this volume contains, we must pronounce it to be one of
the most trustworthy expositions of our social state and
evils which has yet been produced."—*Truth Seeker*,
July, 1849.

The Romifh Church. The Doctrines of the Romifh Church, as exhibited in the NOTES of the DOUAY BIBLE: arranged under feparate heads. By SAMUEL CAPPER. 8vo., price 12s.

"Mr. Capper's book may be regarded as a monument of diligence, of fairnefs, and of Chriftian benevolence; and it will find its way, we doubt not, into the library of every man who wifhes to be informed on what muft, after all, be one of the great controverfies, if not the great controverfy, of the times upon which the Church of CHRIST is entering."—*The Patriot.*

"The work is not only prepared with perfect integrity, but is curious and worthy of place in all libraries, and efpecially of minifters who may have occafion to deal with thefe matters in purfuance of their duties."— *Standard of Freedom.*

"It is a moft valuable contribution to the aids and appliances of that fpecies of religious controverfy which contends *for truth and not for victory,* and ufes the weapons of reafon and charity, not of acrimonious debate and reviling."—*Morning Poft.*

"This is a valuable publication of the Notes of the quarto edition of the Douay Bible, claffified under various heads, fo as to afford an eafy and ready reference on the leading points of doctrine. The notes are taken from the editions of 1633, 1635, and 1816, and are the refult of many years' labours: and the book brings into one's reach an important portion of controverfial matter, which may be ufed with effect in our antagonifm with the errors of the Church of Rome."—*Dublin Chriftian Examiner.*

Portraits in Miniature, or Sketches of Character in Verfe. By HENRIETTA J. FRY, Author of the "Hymns of the Reformation," &c. Illuftrated with Eight Engravings, 8vo., price 10s. 6d.

This little volume holds many a name dear to the beft interefts of fociety, like thofe of Elizabeth Fry, J. J. Gurney, W. Wilberforce, Hannah More, Bifhop Heber, &c.

Fifty Days on Board a Slave Veffel. By the Rev. Pascoe Grenfell Hill, M.A., Chaplain of H.M.S. Cleopatra. Demy 12mo., cloth lettered, price 1s. 6d.

> " This curious and fuccinct narrative gives the experience of a fhort voyage on board one of the flave fhips. We fhall be rejoiced, if the publicity given to this little but intelligent work by our means, affift in drawing the attention of the influential claffes to the fubject."—*Blackwood's Magazine.*
>
> " We hope this little work will have a wide circulation. We can conceive nothing fo likely to do good to the righteous caufe it is intended to promote."— *Examiner.*

The Fugitive Blackfmith, or, Events in the Hiftory of James W. C. Pennington, Paftor of a Prefbyterian Church, New York. Fcap. 8vo., fewed. The fixth thoufand, price 1s.

> " This entrancing narrative * * * We truft that thoufands of our readers will procure the volume, which is publifhed by Mr. Gilpin at a mere trifle—much too cheap to accomplifh the purpofe for which, in part or mainly, it has been publifhed—the raifing a fund to remove the pecuniary burdens which prefs on the author's flock. Nothing short of the sale of Fifty Thousand or Sixty Thousand Copies could be at all availing for this object. * * * We very cordially recommend him and his narrative to the kind confideration of our readers."—*Chriftian Witnefs.*

Cards of Character : a Biographical Game. In a neat cafe, price 5s.

> " This Game, which is prepared by a young Friend, contains much amufement and inftruction. It confifts of brief fketches of the lives and characters of about feventy of the principal perfons of the paft age, and queftions correfponding in number with the Cards. The game is well arranged and very fimple."

The Campaner Thal : or, Difcourfes on the Im-
mortality of the Soul. By JEAN PAUL FR. RICHTER.
Tranflated from the German by JULIETTE BAUER.   Foolf-
cap 8vo., price 2s. 6d.

"—— Report, we regret to fay, is all that we know
of the ' Campaner Thal,' one of Richter's beloved
topics, or rather the life of his whole philofophy,
glimpfes of which look forth on us from almoft every
one of his writings. He died while engaged, under
recent and almoft total blindnefs, in enlarging and re-
modelling this ' Campaner Thal.' The unfinifhed manu-
fcript was borne upon his coffin to the burial vault ; and
Klopftock's hymn, ' Auferftehen wirft du !' 'Thou fhalt
arife, my foul,' ean feldom have been fung with more
appropriate application than over the grave of Jean Paul."
—Carlyle's Mifcellanies.

The Friendly and Feejee Iflands, A Miffionary
Vifit to various Stations in the South Seas, in the year
1847. By the REV. WALTER LAWRY.   With an Appendix,
containing notices of the political conftitution, population,
productions, manners, cuftoms, and mythology of the people, and of the ftate of religion among them.   Edited by
the REV. ELIJAH HOOLE.   12mo., cloth, price 4s. 6d.

" Some of its details of Cannibalifm and Feejeeifm are
very terrible : and that fuch anthropophagi fhould have
been recovered to a common human nature with our-
felves, and to the higher hopes of the Chriftian life, is a
teftimony to revelation which the fceptic may well
ponder."*—Nonconformift.*
" That portion of the narrative relating to the Feejee
Iflands is efpecially worthy of perufal, difplaying as it
does the frightful characteriftics of a fociety in which
habitual and ferocious cannibalifm maintained its ground,
and its gradual tranfition to a more hopeful and fatisfac-
tory condition, in which the 'influence of the prefs'
is already becoming a power for good."*—Morning
Advertifer.*

A Kiss for a Blow. A Collection of Stories for Children, showing them how to prevent quarrelling. By H. C. WRIGHT. Twenty-fifth thousand. 18mo., price 1s.

"Of this little book it is impossible to speak too highly—it is the reflex of the spirit of childhood, full of tenderness, pity, and love: quick to resent, and equally quick to forgive. We wish that all children could imbibe its spirit, then indeed would the world be happier and better."—*Mary Howitt.*

"This volume, of which it were to be wished that every family in the country had a copy, has been reprinted in London by Charles Gilpin; it is an invaluable little book."—*Chambers's Tracts.*

Skyrack; a Fairy Tale. With Six Illustrations Post 8vo., cloth extra, price 2s. 6d.

"It is simply the story of an old oak; but it carries you away to the forest, and refreshes you with its dewy, sunny, solitary life. The spirit of the book is pure as the breezes of the forest themselves. All the imagery, and the whole tone of the story are of that kind which you wish to pervade the mind of your children. In a word, we have rarely enjoyed a more delicious hour, or have been more thoroughly wrapt in sweet, silent, dewy, and balmy forest entrancement, than during the perusal of Skyrack."—*Standard of Freedom.*

Narrative of William W. Brown, an American Slave. Written by Himself. THE ELEVENTH THOUSAND. Fcap. 8vo., price 1s. 6d.

"We would that a copy of this book could be placed in every school library in Massachusetts. We hope and believe that it will be widely circulated."—*Boston Whig.*

"It is an interesting narrative, and should be read by every person in the country. We commend it to the public, and venture the assertion, that no one who takes it up and reads a chapter, will lay it down until he has finished it."—*New Bedford Bulletin.*

"We have read Mr. Brown's Narrative, and found it a thrilling tale."—*Laurence Courier.*

Sparks from the Anvil. By John Burnet.
12mo., fewed. The thirteenth thoufand, price 1s.

"Thefe are fparks indeed of fingular brilliancy."—
Britiſh Friend.

"They deferve to be ftereotyped, and to form part of
the ftandard literature of the age."—*Kentiſh Independent.*

"We fay to all, read it, imbibe its fpirit, and learn
like the writer, to work for and with GOD, towards the
regeneration of your race."—*Nottingham Review.*

"Reader, if you have not read the 'Sparks from the
Anvil,' do fo at once."—*The Echo.*

A Voice from the Forge. By John Burnet.
with a Portrait. Being a fequel to "Sparks from the
Anvil." Seventh thoufand. 12mo., fewed, price 1s.

"In every line coined from the reflecting mind of the
Blackfmith of Maffachufetts, there is a high philofophy
and philanthropy genuine and pure. His fympathies are
univerfal, his afpirations are for the happinefs of all,
and his writings are nervous, terfe, and vigorous."—
London Telegraph.

"The influence of the fmall work before us muft be
for good, and we wifh it every fuccefs. The various
effays it contains are written with natural eloquence, and
contain many juft and original fentiments."—*Scottiſh
Prefs.*

The Paſtor's Wife: or, Devotional Fragments.
From the German of Lavater. By HENRIETTA J. FRY.
18mo., filk, price 2s. 6d.

"This is an exquifite little gem."—*Chriſtian Examiner.*

*** An edition may be obtained with the German appended
to the work, done up in the fame manner, for 3s.

THE PHŒNIX LIBRARY.

The following Series of Original and Reprinted Works, bearing
on the Renovation and Progrefs of Society in Religion,
Morality, and Science, is now in courfe of publication, printed
uniformly, price 2s. 6d. each volume :

Utopia ; or, the Happy Republic.   A Philofophical Romance.   By SIR THOMAS MORE.

Letters on Early Education.   By PESTALOZZI.
With a Memoir of Peftalozzi.

Effects of Civilization on the People in European
States.   By CHARLES HALL, M.D.

The Chriftian Commonwealth.   By JOHN MINTER
MORGAN.   To which is added, AN INQUIRY RESPECTING
PRIVATE PROPERTY, from a Periodical of 1827.

Letters to a Clergyman, on Inftitutions for Ameliorating the Condition of the People, chiefly from Paris,
in the Autumn of 1845.   By the fame Author.

A Tour through Switzerland and Italy, in the years
1846-47.   By the fame Author.

Colloquies on Religion and Religious Education.
By the fame Author.

Tracts.   By the fame Author.

The Revolt of the Bees.   By the fame Author.

The Adventures of Signor Gaudentio Di Lucca.
Attributed to BISHOP BERKELEY.

Effay on St. Paul.   By HANNAH MORE.   2 vols.

Uniform with the above, price 3s. 6d.

Extracts for Schools and Families, in aid of Moral
and Religious Training.

The Prize Effay, on the Ufe and Abufe of Alco-
holic Liquors in health and difeafe. By W. B. CARPENTER,
M.D., F.R.S. Dedicated by permiffion to H. R. H.
Prince Albert. A Prize of One Hundred Guineas having
been offered for the beft Effay on the above fubject, that
fum has juft been awarded to Dr. CARPENTER, by the
Adjudicators, Dr. JOHN FORBES, Dr. G. L. ROUPELL, and
Dr. W. A. GUY. Poft 8vo., price 5s.

"We have now to congratulate the donor and the
public on having obtained an Effay from one of the moft
eminent phyfiologifts."—*Nonconformift.*

"It muft be no fmall fource of gratification to
them (the teetotallers) that the important publication to
which we have been calling the attention of our readers
(the above Effay) fhould find its way to the royal palace,
and that the enlightened Prince, fo diftinguifhed for his
earneftnefs in promoting the beft interefts of his adopted
country, fhould fanction the dedication of the work to
himfelf, and thus confer an honour alike deferved by the
author and his caufe."—*Briftol Mercury.*

William Penn and T. B. Macaulay; being brief
obfervations on 'the charges made in Mr. Macaulay's
"Hiftory of England," against the character of William
Penn. By W. E. FORSTER. 8vo., fewed, price 1s.

Rogerfon's Poems. The Poetical Works of JOHN
BOLTON ROGERSON, author of "Rhyme, Romance, and
Revery, &c."

"His fterling talents are alike a credit to himfelf and
the land of his birth, and we doubt not will fhortly win
for him a foremoft rank among Englifh Poets."—*County
Herald.*

Dymond's Effays on the Principles of Morality, and on the Private and Political Rights and Obligations of Mankind. Royal 8vo., paper cover, price 3s. 6d. Neat emboffed cloth, 4s. 6d.

"The high ftandard of morality to which thefe Effays aim at directing the attention of mankind, juftly entitle them to the extenfive circulation which they have obtained in three previous editions; and the prefent cheap and popular form in which they now appear, having reached a fale of nearly feven thoufand in twelve months, is an unequivocal proof of public approbation."

Hymns of the Reformation. By LUTHER and others. From the German; to which is added his Life from the original Latin of Melancthon, by the Author of "The Paftor's Legacy." 18mo., cloth, price 2s. 6d.; and neatly bound in filk, price 3s. 6d.

An Encyclopædia of Facts, Anecdotes, Arguments, and Illuftrations from Hiftory, Philofophy, and Chriftianity, in fupport of the principles of Permanent and Univerfal Peace. By EDWIN PAXTON HOOD, Author of "Fragments of Thought and Compofition," &c. 18mo., fewed, price 1s. 6d.

The Art of Memory. The new Mnemonic Chart and Guide to the Art of Memory. Neatly Illuf- trated with upwards of 200 Woodcuts, &c. Cloth, price 2s. 6d.

A Selection of Scripture Poetry. By LOVELL SQUIRE. Third Edition, containing many Original Hymns not hitherto publifhed. 18mo., cloth, price 2s. 6d. The fame to be had nicely bound in filk, with gilt edges, 4s.

Poetical Sketches of Scripture Characters.—Abra ham to Job. By MARTHA YARDLEY. Sewed, price 6d.

A Selection from the Writings of JOHN SYDNEY TAYLOR, A.M., Barrister-at-Law. 8vo., cloth, price 12s.

"On this rock we stand—on the adamantine basis of Christian principle we would build the whole fabric of legislation which regards the public morals."—(p. 213.)

"The volume before us is a noble testimony to the worth of the deceased writer."—*Yorkshireman.*

An Interesting Memoir of Three Brothers, (G., J. and S. Peirson) who died of Consumption. 18mo., sewed, price 4d.

The Wells of Scripture. By HENRIETTA J. FRY. Crown 8vo., cloth, price 2s.

"This little work is unpretending in its character; but dwelling as it does on themes of hallowed interest, we can, with satisfaction, recommend it to our readers."

Three Lectures on the Moral Elevation of the People. By THOMAS BEGGS. Price 1s.

"The working classes ought to read them, that they may learn how much power resides in themselves; the middle classes should read them, and learn that wealth confers increased responsibility on its possessor; and even our nobles should read them, that they may learn that the downfal of *false*, and the reign of *true* nobility are alike at hand."—*Nottingham Review.*

"The Lectures are full of large and comprehensive views of man, and the writer aims in every respect to promote his moral elevation."—*Universe.*

Defensive War, proved to be a Denial of Christianity and of the Government of GOD. With illustrative facts and anecdotes. By HENRY C. WRIGHT. 12mo., cloth, price 2s.

The Boy's Own Book. Intended as a Prefent for Children on leaving School. 18mo., ftiff covers, price 6d.

The Young Servant's Book. Intended as a Prefent for Girls on firft going to Service. 18mo., ftiff covers, price 4d.

Waterloo Series. In Seven Numbers, fewed, price 6d. complete. Edited by ELIHU BURRITT.

No. 1. Voice from Waterloo.—The Silver Tankard.
No. 2. Hannibal; or, the Story of a Wafted Life.—The Bower on the Hill.
No. 3. The Story of the Beautiful Book.
No. 4. The Story of Oberlin.
No. 5. The Man that Killed his Neighbours.
No. 6. Soldiers and Citizens.
No. 7. Story of Frank.

William Allen: his Life and Correfpondence. 3 vols. 8vo., price 24s.

"The holieft and lowelieft of Friends."—*Dr. Campbell.*

The Sunday School Teacher. Defigned to aid in elevating and perfecting the Sabbath School Syftem. By the Rev. I. TODD. 12mo., cloth, price 2s. 6d.

"Every Sabbath School Teacher fhould regard it as a privilege to purchafe and carefully read the work."— *Philadelphic Obferver.*

An Argument, drawn from Scripture, to prove that the Miniftry of the Gofpel ought to be entirely Gratuitous. By the late THOMAS WEMEYS. 3rd edition, 12mo., fewed, price 4d.

Gleanings for Children; or, Eafy Stories carefully felected for Young Children. 18mo., fewed, price 6d.

A Voyage to the Slave Coasts of West and East

Africa. **By the Rev. Pascoe Grenfell Hill, R.N.,**
Author of " Fifty Days on Board a Slave Vessel." 12mo.,
cloth lettered, price 1s.

> " This brief but interesting narrative proceeds from
> one who has witnessed the horrors of the Slave-trade,
> as carried on in various parts of the globe. * * * *
> The unpretending style in which the narrative is writ-
> ten, and the stamp of truth which it carries with it,
> induce us to recommend it to an extensive perusal."—
> *Standard of Freedom.*

The Norwegian Sailor : a Sketch of the Life of

George Noscoe. Written by himself. With an introductory
note, by Dr. Raffles. Fifth edition, with an account of
his death. Foolscap 8vo., cloth, price 2s.

> " He (G. Noscoe) was really a remarkable man. I
> would earnestly recommend it to every sailor."—*Dr.*
> *Raffles.*

Speeches of Richard Cobden, Esq., M.P., on

Peace, Financial Reform, Colonial Reform, and other
subjects, delivered during 1849. Foolscap 8vo., 3s. 6d.
cloth, 2s. 6d. sewed.

A Guide to True Peace ; or a Method of at-

taining to inward and Spiritual Prayer. Compiled chiefly
from the writings of Fenelon, Lady Guion, and Michael
Molinos. 32mo., cloth, price 1s.

Hints on Cultivating the Christian Temper. By

the Rev. H. A. Boardman, D.D. Reprinted from the
American edition, 32mo., cloth, price 6d.

Gallic Gleanings. A Series of Letters, descriptive

of two Excursions to the French Metropolis and the
Parisian Peace Congress, 1849. Addressed to a Friend in
London. By A. Nicholson. 18mo., cloth, price 2s. 6d.

Peace Congress. Report of the Proceedings of the Second General Peace Congress, held in Paris on the 22nd, 23rd, and 24th of August, 1849. Compiled from authentic documents.   vo., cloth, price 2s. 6d.

Electoral Districts; or, the Apportionment of the Representation of the Country on the basis of its Population; being an inquiry into the working of the Reform Bill, and into the merits of the representative scheme, by which it is proposed to supersede it.   By ALEXANDER MACKAY.   8vo. Sewed, 1s.

Political Equity; or, a Fair Equalization of the National Burdens, comprised in some intermingled and scattered thoughts, suggesting an anti-destitution policy, a graduated system of taxation on real property and income, &c.   By THEOPHILUS WILLIAMS.   8vo., sewed, price 2s.

Reminiscences of Poland; her Revolutions and her Rights. A brief sketch of the causes of the revolutions, from 1839 to the incorporation of Cracow with the Austrian Empire; with a short local description of Cracow, By ISIDORE LIVINSKY, a Polish refugee.   Foolscap 8vo., cloth, 2s.; sewed, 1s. 6d.

Parables: translated from the German of KRUM-MACHER. Containing the Hyacinth; the Persian, the Jew, and the Christian; Asaph and Heman; Life and Death; the Mother's Faith, &c.   16mo., sewed, price 1s.

The Peace Reading Book; being a series of Selections from the Sacred Scriptures, the Early Christian Fathers, and Historians, Philosophers and Poets,—the wise and thoughtful of all ages; condemnatory of the principles and practice of war, inculcating those of true Christianity. Edited by H. G. ADAMS.   12mo., cloth, price 2s.

Gleanings from Pious Authors. Comprising the Wheatsheaf, Fruits and Flowers, Garden, and Shrubbery. With a brief notice of the former publications of these volumes. By JAMES MONTGOMERY. A new edition. Foolscap 8vo., price 3s.

Hymns and Meditations. By A. L. W. Sewed. gilt edges, 1s. Silk, gilt edges, 2s. 6d.

How Little Henry of Eichenfels came to the Knowledge of GOD.

" It is interesting to observe, that the translation of this little book (from the German) is the effort of young persons who have willingly sacrificed some hours of recreation to aid the cause of humanity.

The Voyage Companion : a Parting Gift to Female Emigrants. By the Author of "A Word on behalf of a Slave," &c. &c. Foolscap 8vo., price 6d.

H.R.H. Prince Albert's Prize. A Plea for the Right against Might, or the Temporal Advantages of the Sabbath to the Labouring Classes. By JOHN COBLEY, Foolscap 8vo., price 6d.

The Soldier's Destiny. A Tale of the Times. The Enlistment.—Leaving Home.—The Deserter.—The Battle.—The Night after the Battle.—The Return. By GEORGE WALLER. Foolscap 8vo., price 1s.

Memoirs of Paul Cuffe, a Man of Colour, Compiled from authentic sources. By WILSON ARMISTED. 18mo., cloth, price 1s.

" The exertions of this truly benevolent individual entitle him to the esteem of the world, and the grateful remembrance of latest posterity."

PORTRAITS.

Elizabeth Fry. A full-length Portrait of Elizabeth Fry. Engraved by SAMUEL COUSINS, A.R.A. from a picture by George Richmond.

	l.	*s.*
Artifts' proof . .	10	10
Proofs with autographs .	7	7
Proofs	4	4
Prints	2	2

Elizabeth Fry : Engraved on Copper. By BLOOD, from a painting by Leflie.

	s.	*d.*
Proofs	15	0
Prints	7	6

Thomas Clarkfon. A very fplendid Portrait of this diftinguifhed philanthropift.

	l.	*s.*	*d.*
India proofs, firft clafs .	1	0	0
Second clafs . .		10	6
Prints		5	0

William Allen. Drawn on Stone. By DAY and HAGHE, from a painting by Dickfee.

	l.	*s.*	*d.*
India proofs, firft clafs .	1	10	0
Second clafs . .	1	1	0
Prints . . .		10	6

Samuel Gurney. Drawn on Stone by Dickfee.

	s.	*d.*
Firft clafs . . .	10	0
Prints	5	0

CPSIA information can be obtained
at www.ICGtesting.com
Printed in the USA
BVHW041656240419
546434BV00015B/163/P